Differentiated Instructional Strategies

in Practice
Training, Implementation, and Supervision

Differentiated Instructional Strategies

in Practice
Training, Implementation, and Supervision

Gayle H. Gregory

CORWIN PRESS, INC.
A Sage Publications Company
Thousand Oaks, California

For information:

Corwin Press, Inc.
A Sage Publications Company
2455 Teller Road
Thousand Oaks, California 91320
www.corwinpress.com

Sage Publications Ltd.
6 Bonhill Street
London EC2A 4PU
United Kingdom

Sage Publications India Pvt. Ltd.
B-42, Panchsheel Enclave
Post Box 4109
New Delhi 110 017 India

Printed in the United States of America

Library of Congress Cataloging-in-Publication Data

Gregory, Gayle.
Differentiated instructional strategies in practice : training, implementation, and supervision / Gayle H. Gregory.
    p. cm.
Includes bibliographical references and index.
ISBN 0-7619-3901-6 (Cloth) — ISBN 0-7619-3902-4 (Paper)
    1. Individualized instruction. 2. Teachers—In-service training. I. Title.
LB1031G735 2003
371.39′4—dc211

                              2003002562

This book is printed on acid-free paper.

Illustrations from *Differentiated Instructional Strategies: One Size Doesn't Fit All* (Thousand Oaks: Corwin Press, 2002) are by Tammy Kay Brunson, Thomson, GA 30824.

Acquiring Editor:	Faye Zucker
Corwin Editorial Assistant:	Stacy Wagner
Production Editor:	Sanford Robinson
Copy Editor:	Pam Suwinsky
Typesetter:	C&M Digitals (P) Ltd.
Proofreader:	Toni Williams
Indexer:	Karen McKenzie
Cover Designer:	Tracy E. Miller
Production Artist:	Lisa Miller

Contents

Acknowledgments

I am indebted to many professional educators for their work, writings, and examples. Those whose influence can be seen in this book include Carolyn Chapman, Pat Wolfe, Howard Gardner, Daniel Goleman, David Sousa, Bob Sylwester, Eric Jensen, Tony Gregorc, Bernice McCarthy, Carol Rolheiser, Bob Marzano, Jay McTighe, Carol Ann Tomlinson, Carol O'Connor, Pam Robbins, Rita King, Robin Fogarty, and Kay Burke, to mention a few. A special thanks goes to friend and colleague Joanne Quinn for her ongoing enthusiasm and support.

I thank my family members for their love and support and offer special thanks to my husband Joe for his understanding, encouragement, and ideas during the long hours of writing, listening, and editing.

About the Author

 **Gayle H. Gregory** has been a teacher in elementary, middle, and secondary schools. For many years, she taught in schools with extended periods of instructional time (block schedules). She has had extensive districtwide experience as a curriculum consultant and staff development coordinator. Most recently, she was course director at York University for the Faculty of Education, teaching in the teacher education program. She now consults internationally (Europe, Asia, North and South America, Australia) with teachers, administrators, and staff developers in the areas of managing change, differentiated instruction, brain-compatible learning, block scheduling, emotional intelligence, instructional and assessment practices, cooperative group learning, presentation skills, renewal of secondary schools, enhancing teacher quality, and coaching and mentoring.

Gayle is affiliated with many organizations, including the Association for Supervision and Curriculum Development and the National Staff Development Council. She is the coauthor of *Designing Brain-Compatible Learning; Thinking Inside the Block Schedule: Strategies for Teaching in Extended Periods of Time;* and *Differentiated Instructional Strategies: One Size Doesn't Fit All.* She has been featured in Video Journal of Education's best-selling elementary and secondary videos *Differentiating Instruction to Meet the Needs of All Learners.*

Gayle is committed to lifelong learning and professional growth for herself and others. She may be contacted by e-mail at gregorygayle@ netscape.net. Her Web site is www3.sympatico.ca/gayle.gregory.

Introduction

ADULTS NEED DIFFERENTIATED LEARNING OPPORTUNITIES TOO

This book is intended to assist school administrators and staff developers in strengthening the concept of differentiated instruction in schools and classrooms to better meet the individual and diverse needs of students.

It is apparent to many of us who train teachers that adults need differentiated learning opportunities just as children do, because adults begin at different places based on their backgrounds, experiences, abilities, and interests. Thus, this book covers the basic elements of differentiated instruction as well as how teachers and staff developers as a professional learning community can focus on those principles.

Part I highlights the attributes and research of quality staff development and job-embedded training strategies, including book study, video and popcorn sessions, and action research.

Part II offers a chapter-by-chapter series of activities and discussion starters based on the book *Differentiated Instructional Strategies: One Size Doesn't Fit All* (Gregory & Chapman, 2002a) that will facilitate training with a book study group or as individual activities at faculty meetings.

Part III examines teacher approaches to change, using familiar tools such as the Concerns Based Adoption Model (C.B.A.M.; Hord, Rutherford, Huling-Austin, & Hall, 1987) and adopter types (Rogers, 1995) ranging from Innovators to Resistors. Coaching and supervision using observation tools for the differentiated classroom are covered, and an implementation profile is offered to assess where members of the learning community are in the process of adapting to differentiated instructional strategies.

Part I

Building School Capacity Through Professional Development

Chapter I-1

School Capacity and Student Achievement

Educational policies and programs for professional development should support school capacity for change and improvement, according to Newmann, King, and Youngs (2000). School improvement and capacity for change are dependent upon multiple factors:

- Teachers' knowledge, skills, and dispositions *thus* quality staff development
- Professional learning communities *thus* collaborative learning
- Program coherence *thus* consensus and focus
- Technical resources *thus* materials and training
- Principal leadership *thus* support and encouragement

All of these elements are necessary to improve the quality of instruction, curriculum, and assessment in order to increase student achievement. Principals and teacher leaders who want to improve conditions that build school capacity must focus on these components, evaluating evidence of them in their schools as they develop learning organizations that can manage and sustain change (see Figure 1).

Figure 1   Influences on school capacity and student achievement

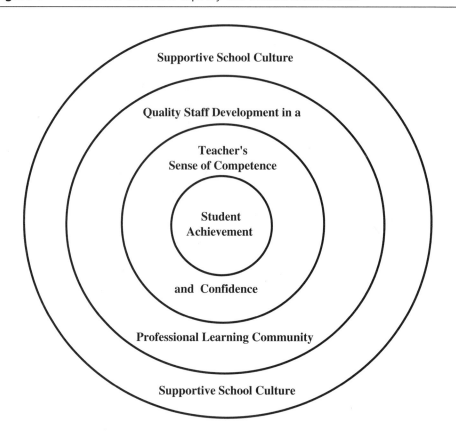

Supportive School Culture

Quality Staff Development in a

Teacher's
Sense of Competence

Student
Achievement

and Confidence

Professional Learning Community

Supportive School Culture

ESSENTIAL ELEMENTS FOR BUILDING SCHOOL CAPACITY FOR CHANGE

Student Achievement. At the heart of school improvement is student achievement. Everything we do in schools should be focused on increasing students' knowledge and skills.

Teachers' Sense of Competence and Confidence. Teachers who are not valued and respected often do not feel comfortable or empowered enough to make the changes necessary to improve student learning. Those teachers who feel that they are incapable or lack the skills to differentiate instruction need continual support, encouragement, and reinforcement of their efforts so that they have the will and skill to succeed in differentiating instruction.

Quality Staff Development in a Professional Learning Community and a Supportive School Culture. A teacher's sense of efficacy (Guskey, 1994) is what a teacher believes he or she can do to effect student learning. Thus the same safe, supportive climate that we want in the classroom for students must also be created for the adult learners in the school community. People who enjoy their work and find their workplace pleasant, non-threatening, yet challenging usually feel more confident than those who don't. They are able to take the risks involved in order to learn and develop new skills and strategies.

"Emotional hijacking" (Goleman, 1995), which causes people to react emotionally to stress, threat, or fatigue, makes them feel helpless and unable to think rationally. That is not what we want for learners, whether they are age 5 or age 45. Adults in a state of relaxed alertness are more confident and more open to new learning and change, just as their students are. Treating adult learners with the same respect that we want for our students only models good practice.

POWERFUL STAFF DEVELOPMENT SUPPORTS CHANGE AND INNOVATION

Professional Development is about change—change in what you know and believe about teaching and learning and in what you can do in the classroom. Part of bringing about real change is creating a context or climate in which change is less difficult.

—David Collins, 1998

In *A New Vision for Staff Development* (1997), Sparks and Hirsh point out that powerful staff development supports innovation, experimentation, and collegial sharing. Staff development has real impact when it engages people in daily planning, critiquing, and problem solving, and when it provides ongoing practice-based assistance. Powerful staff development deepens the content knowledge, instructional skills, and assessment skills that help teachers regularly monitor student learning.

Powerful professional development is also *results-driven* staff development, connected to what students need to know and be able to do. It provides educators with the knowledge and skills they need to ensure student success related to targeted standards, competencies, and expectations.

The content of staff development sessions should be focused on that body of knowledge and skills necessary to produce greater success for students, recognizing that adults need to learn in ways that are comfortable and engaging for them. The school and its organizational structures should support adult learning within the context of the professional learning community.

PROFESSIONAL LEARNING COMMUNITIES

The most promising strategy for sustained, substantive school improvement is developing the ability of school personnel to function as professional learning communities.

—Richard DuFour & Robert Eaker, 1998

Professional learning communities change the climate and purpose of professional dialogue between and among teachers. Dialogue differs from discussion because dialogue increases the depth of understanding of ideas and concepts.

The purposes of a professional learning community (Murphy & Lick, 2001) include:

- Developing a deeper understanding of academic content
- Supporting the implementation of curricula and instructional initiatives
- Identifying a focus for the school's instructional process
- Studying research on teaching and learning
- Monitoring the impact of instructional initiatives on students
- Examining student work

Administrators who want to cultivate professional learning communities within their schools can use the following checklist (adapted from Collins, 1998) to identify activities that cultivate and sustain a professional learning community:

CREATING AND SUSTAINING A PROFESSIONAL LEARNING COMMUNITY

___ Do teachers talk regularly about teaching and learning?

___ Do teachers have opportunities to observe each other teach?

___ Do teachers examine student work and solve problems collaboratively about the next steps in the learning process?

___ Are there opportunities for book studies or action research facilitated by teachers or administrators?

___ Do teachers have shared planning time to develop lessons and share strategies during the school day?

___ Do teachers have time to examine data to determine how students are progressing?

___ Are there opportunities to play as well as work together?

___ Do people give advice as well as ask for suggestions?

___ Do teachers share and support one another's efforts?

___ Is training and developing new skills and knowledge a collegial experience where teachers can share a common language, implement together, and coach one another?

___ Do teachers participate in setting the school's focus for differentiation?
___ Is collective decision making part of the process of designing staff development?

In the words of Peter Senge (1990), "We must build organizations where people continuously expand their capacity to create the results they truly desire, where new and expansive patterns of thinking are nurtured, where collective aspiration is set free, and where people are continually learning together."

School Culture

The culture of an enterprise plays the dominant role in exemplary performance.

—Terrence E. Deal &
Kent D. Peterson, 1999

The culture of the school facilitates or inhibits its evolution to a professional learning organization. Deal and Peterson (1999) suggest that culture includes a shared mission and purpose within which people work, and it includes the norms, values, and beliefs that make up the fabric of the school.

The school's mission and purpose come from the held values, beliefs, assumptions, and norms embraced by its faculty. *Values* are what the organization stands for, that which gives the work a deeper meaning. *Beliefs* are what we understand and believe as truth. *Assumptions* are created through dialogue that facilitates shared values and beliefs. *Norms* are those stated or unstated group behaviors that all members expect to be upheld in their interactions.

Examples of positive norms include:

- Everyone's ideas are respected.
- Everyone has a voice and opinion.
- Everyone is positive in talking about the school and students.
- Everyone is entitled to support and help.

Examples of negative norms include:

- Put down rather than put up.
- Pretend to be involved.
- Criticism and complaints are okay.
- Powerful negative leaders.

Figure 2 Training, implementation, and transfer to teacher's repertoire (adapted from Joyce & Showers, 1985)

Level of Impact

Components of Training	Awareness Plus Concept Understanding	Skill Attainment	Application/ Problem Solving
Presentation of Theory	85%	15%	5-10%
Modeling of the Innovation	85%	18%	5-10%
Practice and Low-Risk Feedback	85%	80%	10-15%
Coaching Study Teams Peer Visits	90%	90%	80-90 %

Principals and staff developers must take every opportunity to create dialogue that will lead teachers toward a more positive school culture in which shared vision and mission can prevail and influence actions.

LEARNING AND IMPLEMENTATION

Joyce and Showers (1995) reported that the levels of transfer increase based on the type of learning experiences and training in which people are involved.

Being exposed only to theory and modeling results in very little actual application in the classroom, whereas those teachers who have opportunities to practice in risk-free conditions increase their skill level considerably. Further, teachers who are in collaborative situations with a coaching component that includes study teams and opportunities to problem-solve with supportive colleagues have an 80–90 percent chance of applying the innovation into their classroom repertoire. Thus the power of job-embedded learning.

Figure 2 displays the percentages of awareness, skill attainment, and application that can be expected from the following components of staff development training:

- Presentation of theory
- Modeling of the innovation
- Practice and feedback
- Impact of coaching, study teams, and peer interaction

Note that inservice training, workshops, and how-to-do-it's are all useful and important in the change process, as is the opportunity to practice in safe environments, but most profound of all is the necessity for ongoing dialogue with coaches, peers, and study teams. Sharing, problem solving, and collaborative supports are essential to facilitate implementation and transfer into the classroom and into a teacher's repertoire.

Chapter I-2

Job-Embedded Strategies for Differentiated Professional Development

It is now recognized that learning within the schoolhouse during working hours is a powerful experience for educators. To sustain a professional learning community, this job-embedded learning must be an ongoing activity.

Some of the purposes served by job-embedded staff development include:

- Developing a deeper understanding of content and increasing teachers' knowledge base
- Supporting implementation of curricular, instructional, and assessment initiatives
- Providing coherence and focus to school growth and improvement
- Focusing on a specific, targeted schoolwide need
- Continuing the professional dialogue about teaching and learning

Strategies to accomplish job-embedded staff development include:

- Study groups
- Coaching
- Cadres
- Video viewing
- Journaling
- Jigsaw strategy
- Action research
- Portfolios
- Curriculum development
- Examining student work
- Mentoring
- Cases

Any of these job-embedded learnings should focus on increasing student achievement through deeper understanding of academic content and increased instructional initiatives. These learnings should support schoolwide needs and continue the study of teaching and learning while monitoring their impact. Time for collegial dialogue is always an essential component of job-embedded staff development. Some of the most effective job-embedded strategies that can be used to explore differentiated instruction include study groups, video viewing, the jigsaw strategy, action research, and teacher inquiry (see Powerful Designs, 1999).

STUDY GROUPS

What Are Study Groups?

Study groups are an opportunity to dialogue around meaningful information about teaching and learning. In dialogue, the goal is deeper meaning and understanding. It focuses on inquiry, reflection, and exploration. A journal article or a book chapter about teacher needs to support student learning may be selected as a focus of the group. Part II of this volume provides guidelines for using *Differentiated Instructional Strategies: One Size Doesn't Fit All* (Gregory & Chapman, 2002a) as such a focus.

Why Participate in Study Groups?

Teachers in study groups get a chance to peruse research and current information about teaching and learning. They are able to explore effective instructional strategies and other resources. Teachers may examine new skills and dialogue around their use in the classrooms with students. During a study group session, teachers may also set goals and create plans for implementation.

Figure 3   Advanced organizer for study group

An Idea That Interested Me	How It Was Used	How I Could Use It	Notes
An Idea That Interested Me			
An Idea That Interested Me			
An Idea That Interested Me			

How Do We Facilitate a Study Group?

1. Select a book chapter or journal article that may be pre-read or perhaps organized as a jigsaw (see 'Jigsaw Strategy' following) during the study group session. Many teachers don't have time to read prior to the session, and a jigsaw facilitates learning when pre-reading is impossible.

2. Appoint someone to prepare an advanced organizer to help focus discussion and to record key ideas (Figure 3).

3. Assign roles to each member of the group. Roles may include Recorder, Questioner, Clarifier, Encourager, Timekeeper, Facilitator, and Summarizer. Figure 4 offers helpful language that can help group members fill each of these roles.

4. Develop questions that ensure that dialogue is focused and purposeful. Encourage all members of the group to pose questions for dialogue that would interest and benefit themselves and others.

Figure 4   Bookmarks may be given to people in study groups so that they have helpful language to use when performing their roles (adapted from Robbins, Gregory, & Herndon, 2000)

Encourager	Questioner	Clarifier
Helpful language:	*Helpful language:*	*Helpful language:*
Great idea Thanks for sharing What do you think? Fine idea Right on... what else... Thank you...	Who could...? What's a first step? How could we...? What's the best plan? When can we...? Any ideas...?	Is this what... Explain to me Say again... Did I hear... I think you said... It sounds to me...

Summarizer	Recorder	Facilitator
Helpful language:	*Helpful language:*	*Helpful language:*

I think we agree
that...
Most of us said...
Some of us...
Others differ...
It seems to me...
In summary...
	Perhaps...
	I think...
	My idea...
	Suppose...
	Another idea...
	Anyone else...
		Whose turn is it?
		Has everyone given
		   an idea?
		We have___ minutes
		That's 3 done, we
		   have ___ more to
		   do.
		What do you think?
		Are we ready to move
		   on?

5. Ask group members to set goals and predict the impact of trying some of the ideas or commit to further exploration of the ideas discovered.

6. Ask group members to incorporate journaling and reflective organizers as they explore some of the ideas from the study group in their classroom practice. A focus from the study group can often lead to action research to investigate the impact of a particular technique or strategy in greater depth.

POPCORN AND A VIDEO

What Is Video Viewing?

Videos provide an opportunity for teachers to view classrooms in action, and to hear and see new research and innovative processes that can be used in their own classrooms and schools. It has been said that a picture is worth a thousand words. Seeing techniques used by real teachers with real students is exciting and breeds confidence in other teachers. Some videos may also provide research and background information from experts and master teachers.

Why View Videos?

Videos are a powerful way to spark discussion about teaching and learning and actually see teachers working in classrooms with students. Teachers do not often have a chance to observe other teachers or to analyze and/or critique the teaching process. Videos offer them a chance to question the rationale behind the instructional and assessment processes that teachers select. They bring each strategy to life and let teachers see other teachers using it successfully. They also illustrate student behavior with a particular strategy or technique, and they provide a way of seeing and hearing experts share research and innovations that merit consideration.

How Do We Facilitate Video Viewing?

1. Prepare an advanced organizer to collect key issues or information. See Figure 5 for a sample that uses de Bono's (1987) Thinking CorT strategies Plus, Minus, and Interesting, or Figure 6 for the Six-Lenses-for-Examination method adapted from de Bono's (1999) *Six Hats Thinking*.

2. View the video.

3. Facilitate the dialogue following the video viewing. If participants used Plus-Minus-Interesting (Figure 5) or Six Lenses for Examination (Figure 6), those headings can be used to organize the dialogue. Other advance organizers can also provide the framework for discussion.

4. Consider possible applications and ideas.

5. As a group, decide on the next steps, such as reading an article, viewing another video, trying an idea, or attending a workshop or conference.

6. Arrange a follow-up meeting time.

7. Suggest that viewers also record their personal reflections (Figure 7).

Figure 5   Advanced organizer for video viewing (adapted from de Bono, 1987)

Plus: What are the positives that you noticed?		How could you use this?
Minus: What do you have concerns about or do not agree with?		What would you do differently?
Interesting: What did you find insightful or intriguing?		Next steps for you:

Figure 6   Six Lenses for Examination (adapted from de Bono, 1999)

Viewers select one lens to use as they view the video, and they bring that information to the dialogue that follows the viewing.

Clear Lens: What are the facts?

Red Lens: What feeling do these ideas evoke?

Blue Lens: What reflections might you have?

Cloudy Lens: What might be the downside of these ideas?

Green Lens: What are the creative possibilities that may be explored?

Yellow Lens: What are the positives that may be involved?

JIGSAW STRATEGY

What Is Jigsaw?

The jigsaw is a way to read a journal article or book chapter, view a video, or learn new information interdependently with a small group of colleagues.

Figure 7   Personal reflection journal

One idea that interests me is …	Something I'd like to try …
One step I can take tomorrow is …	I wonder …

Why Use Jigsaw?

The jigsaw strategy (Aronson, 1978; Slavin, 1994) is a useful way for staff to learn or explore new information in a way that encourages dialogue and fosters interdependence among faculty as they discuss implications of new innovations or research for their classrooms. It also helps with fostering a more inclusive culture as teachers depend on others for their contributions to complete the group's thinking.

How Do We Facilitate the Jigsaw Strategy?

1. Find two or three journal articles or one article with enough information to divide into three or four sections.

2. Divide the staff into home-base groups of three to five members depending on the number of articles or sections to be read.

3. Assign each staff member in the base group a section to read (10 to 15 minutes of independent reading).

4. Have people who have read the same section form small expert groups to discuss key aspects or issues from their article (15 to 20 minutes).

Figure 8 Advanced organizer for jigsaw

1. Article or section _____	Ideas/Reactions Aha's
2. Article or section _____	Ideas/Reactions Aha's
3. Article or section _____	Ideas/Reactions Aha's
4. Article or section _____	Ideas/Reactions Aha's

5. Have experts return to their base groups and invite each person to share the key points from their reading and discussion with the other members of the group (20 to 30 minutes), using an advance organizer to jot down information that is important to them and their work (Figures 8 and 9).

Figure 9   Jigsaw strategy to enhance interdependence among expert learners

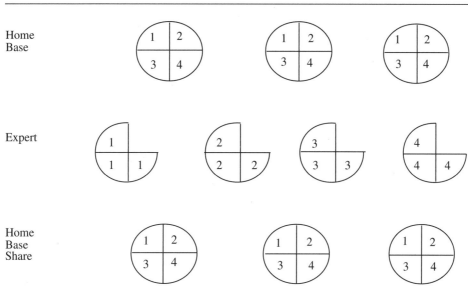

6. Facilitate a large group discussion identifying implications of this information for students and the school.

7. Make some decisions about the next steps for training and implementation.

ACTION RESEARCH

What Is Action Research?

Just as with younger learners, teachers have burning questions that they are curious about. As its name implies, action research is a way to use research and inquiry actively in teachers' daily work in classrooms and schools.

Why Do Action Research?

Action research gives teachers an opportunity to investigate subjects that are near and dear to the heart, to pursue personal interests or quests related to teaching and learning.

How Do We Facilitate Action Research?

1.   A teacher or teachers create a question relevant to their students and their classroom concerning differentiation. Sample questions may include:

- Does a positive climate really make a difference for learners?
- Does pre-assessment data influence my planning and result in adjustable assignments?

2.   A research plan of action is created. This plan should include:

- How will I establish a baseline?
- What data will be collected?
- How will the data be collected? By whom? When?
- How will the data be analyzed? By whom? When?
- How will the findings be shared?

3.   The teacher individually or collaboratively with colleagues refines the research question and plan.

4.   The research is conducted according to the plan outlined in Step 3. Teachers may want to use a time and task agenda (Figure 10), a reflective journal, or a double-duty log (Figure 11) to record information and reflections.

5.   The teacher analyzes the data and shares the findings with colleagues using a report, presentation, or other method. Richard Sagor's *How to Conduct Collaborative Action Research* (1992) provides a detailed discussion of this model for facilitating action research. Teachers may also find the Basic Inquiry Model flowchart (Figure 12) useful for working through the inquiry process.

BAGEL BREAKFAST

A wonderful administrator in Clark County (Las Vegas), Nevada, invites staff to a bagel breakfast every Tuesday morning. There is always a focus or theme for the breakfast. Sometimes it is an instructional strategy, a guest speaker, video viewing, problem solving, article discussion, or a mini-presentation from a staff member. Anyone may attend, including parents.

One Tuesday I was fortunate enough to attend. Beth had been using one of my books for book study, and she asked if I would do a mini-session on graphic organizers. We focused on three: the Venn diagram, the matrix, and the mind map.

Beth challenged teachers to think of a way to use one of those organizers on that day while it was fresh in their minds. As I visited classrooms throughout

Figure 10 Personal agenda to keep track of time and tasks

❁❁❁ A Personal Agenda ❁❁❁

My Agenda (name): ______________________________
Beginning on (date): ______________________________

Dates:	Student Tasks	Log How I used my time:	Reflections	Completion date Teacher & Student Sign-off

SOURCE: Gayle H. Gregory and Carolyn Chapman, *Differentiated Instructional Strategies: One Size Doesn't Fit All.* Thousand Oaks, CA: Corwin Press, © 2002. Reproduction authorized only for the local school site that has purchased this book. www.corwinpress.com

the day, I was excited to see the kindergarten children with hula hoops comparing and contrasting, and first-grade students using a matrix for character, plot, and setting for story writing. Sixth graders were creating mind maps to show the interesting aspects of Nevada. At the next meeting, teachers

Figure 11 Double-duty log

Facts or Ideas	Thoughts and Reflections

SOURCE: Gayle H. Gregory and Carolyn Chapman, *Differentiated Instructional Strategies: One Size Doesn't Fit All.* Thousand Oaks, CA: Corwin Press, © 2002. Reproduction authorized only for the local school site that has purchased this book. www.corwinpress.com

brought examples of student work that used graphic organizers and discussed their use and their students' learnings.

This principal never missed a chance to help teachers stretch their thinking and get better at their craft. Any principal or teacher leader can also use this strategy at different times of day, for example, Wednesday for Lunch or Tea at Four. Figure 13 offers a reflection piece that may be used for metacognition after one of these sessions.

Figure 12   Flowchart for a basic inquiry model for action research

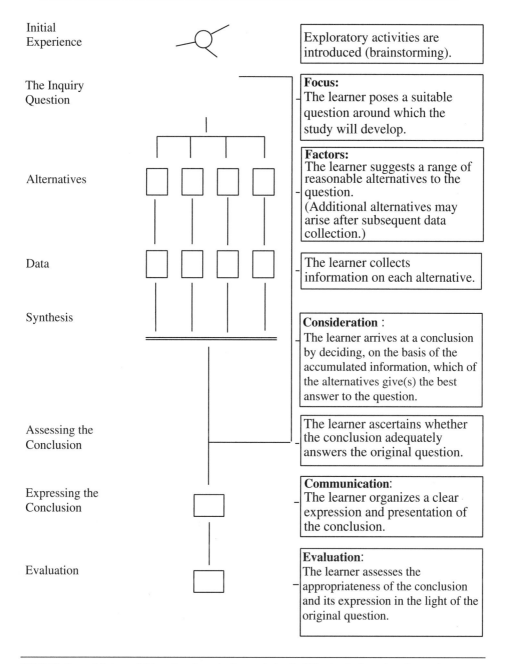

SOURCE: From *Ministry of Education, Ontario, Research Study Skills: Curriculum Ideas for Teachers* (Toronto: Ministry of Education, 1979, p. 20).

Figure 13   Shaping up a review

Four ideas I can consider are …

Three points of clarification are …

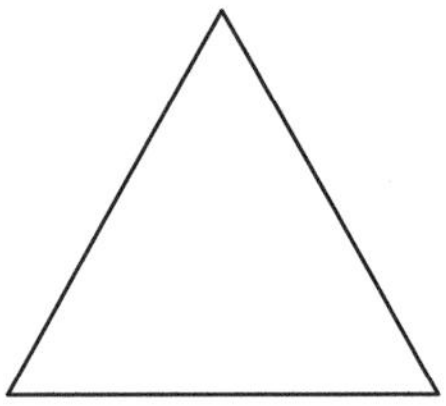

A question that is still going around in my mind!

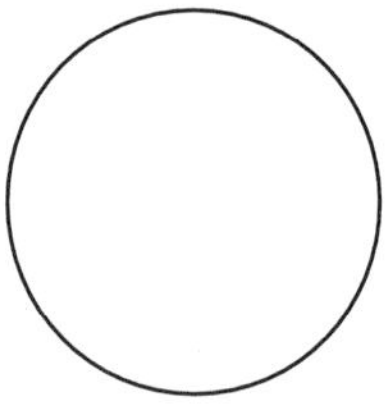

Part II

Book Study Using *Differentiated Instructional Strategies: One Size Doesn't Fit All* and Other Training Resources

II-Introduction

One Size Doesn't Fit All

DIFFERENTIATED INSTRUCTION: CONCEPT CLARIFICATION

To begin, let's consider the definition of *differentiation* and how to promote that shared vision between and among faculty. Differentiation is a philosophy that enables teachers to plan strategically in order to reach the needs of the diverse learners in classrooms today. Differentiation is not just a set of instructional tools but a philosophy that a teacher and a professional learning community embrace to reach the unique needs of every learner.

Prior to reading *Differentiated Instructional Strategies: One Size Doesn't Fit All* (Gregory & Chapman, 2002a) or embarking on the journey of differentiated instruction, invite teachers to participate in a Four Corner activity using Figure 14.

Four Corners

Each teacher takes a few minutes to finish the prompts in each quadrant of the Four Corners form. Then they are invited to walk about the room sharing their ideas with other teachers. This helps teachers open mental files and develop a shared language about differentiation.

Four Corners also serves as a pre-assessment, so that the levels of understanding, commitment, and current practices as well as the needs of teachers are evident. This pre-assessment strategy can also be used with students to find out what they already know about a topic, what they are interested in, and which concepts are clear or are still in need of

Figure 14 Four Corners

I think it is …	A symbol for it might be …
I think it's important because …	
I already meet the needs of my students by …	I need to know …

clarification. Four Corners also promotes dialogue and interaction among learners and can be used as a focus activity at the beginning of a new topic or as a review before a test.

Brainstorming Options

Following Four Corners, teachers may participate in a brainstorming session using Figure 15 to identify the basic concepts of differentiated instruction and to identify their options for differentiation.

Figure 15 Options for differentiated instruction

How do learners differ?

—

—

—

—

—

—

How and what can we differentiate?

—

—

—

—

—

Faculty Meetings as Professional Learning Communities

Often faculty meetings are just a litany of information and paper pushing and have very little to do with professional learning and student achievement. Taking just the first 20 minutes of a faculty meeting to focus on differentiation serves to keep teachers' eyes on the target, to emphasize the coherence of the initiative, to support the process, and to provide resources for implementation.

The strategies that follow may be used for a book study group or individually as staff meeting activities to keep the focus and to support implementation. Most of the training strategies are based on the book *Differentiated Instructional Strategies: One Size Doesn't Fit All* (Gregory & Chapman, 2002a), and the text that follows contains cross-references in parentheses to the relevant pages in that book.

Book study is an excellent job-embedded training strategy that facilitates dialogue and helps build a professional learning community. Video viewing is also an important training strategy, and some of the activities that follow refer to video training resources by Tomlinson (1998b) and by Gregory and Chapman (2002b, 2002c).

WHY DIFFERENTIATION? (PAGES X–XI)

Using Graphic Organizers to Connect Concepts

After reading the book's Introduction, teachers may work in small groups to create a word web with differentiation as the central theme (Figure 16). Word webs are graphic organizers that are verbal or linguistic in nature. Word webs place the concept in the center of the web as a theme, and elements related to the concept branch out from the center.

Mind maps differ from word webs in that they use words and symbolic visual representation rather than words alone. They are useful in demonstrating understanding of a concept and visually depicting a complete connection of ideas and elements. An alternative strategy to creating a word web or mind map would be to ask teachers to use Figure 17 to create a pie chart that depicts the attributes of a differentiated classroom and describes what it looks like, sounds like, and feels like.

Collegial Problem Solving During Implementation

It is helpful for teachers to identify their concerns about differentiation so that they can be responded to appropriately. The following strategy may be used to help teachers voice their concerns in a safe environment and also to open up problem-solving dialogue and encourage collegial support during implementation.

Three-Step Problem Solution Seeking

- In supportive groups of three, ask teachers to letter off A, B, and C.
- As Step 1, *Person A* will share a concern or problem that is related to differentiated instruction.
- As Step 2, *Person B* will question and clarify the problem and then brainstorm possibilities for solving the situation.
- As Step 3, *Person C* will listen and record all the ideas, and perhaps suggest one that they think shows promise.
- Ultimately, Person A will decide on the one suggestion that might work for them and describe how they might utilize it (adapted from Bennett, Rolheiser-Bennett, & Stevahn, 1991).

The roles can be rotated within the group so that everyone gets a chance to have his or her problem solved and everyone can help suggest

Figure 16   Word webs can be used to organize data, demonstrate understanding of major concepts, and make connections between concepts (Parry & Gregory, 1998)

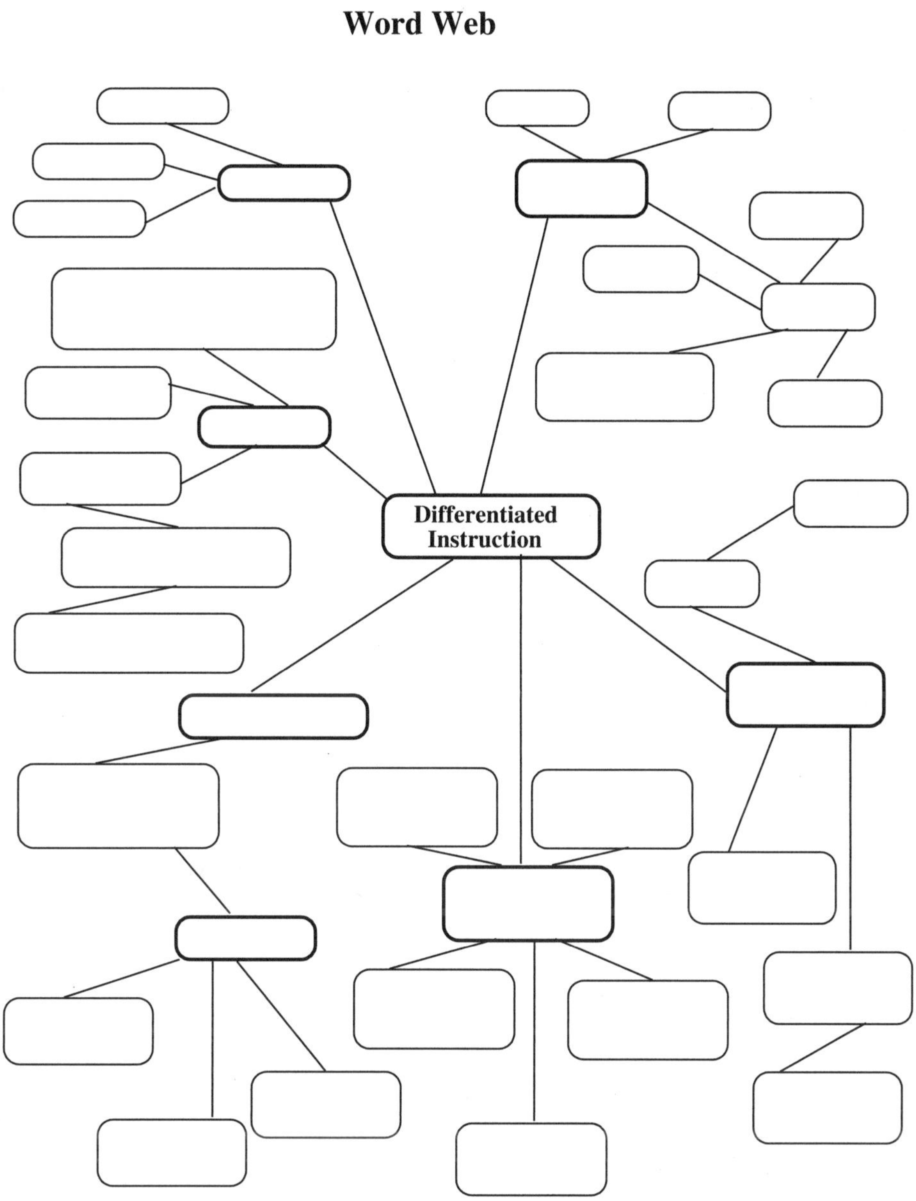

Word Web

Figure 17   A pie chart shows attributes of a differentiated classroom

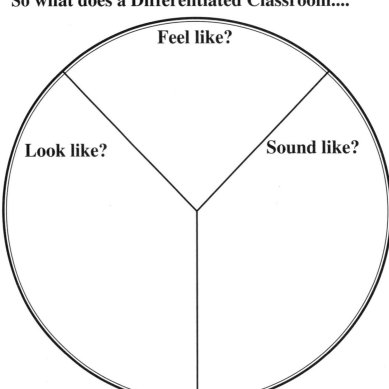

So what does a Differentiated Classroom....

Feel like?

Look like?

Sound like?

solutions to others in the group. This strategy reinforces the "collective wisdom" housed in each faculty and also strengthens collegial bonds of support that foster a professional learning community.

PLANNING FOR DIFFERENTIATED INSTRUCTION (PAGES XII–XIV)

Using the Framework

Present the six-column framework for differentiated instruction (Figure 18), suggesting that if we are trying to understand and create classrooms in

Figure 18 Framework for designing differentiated classrooms

Climate	Knowing the Learner	Assessing the Learner	Adjustable Assignments	Instructional Strategies	Curriculum Approaches

• Safe
• Nurturing
• Encourages risk taking
• Inclusive
• Multi-sensory
• Stimulating
• Complex
• Challenging
• Collaborative
 	
• Questioning
• Cubing
 	
Team and Class Building
 	
Norms
	• **Learning styles**
	
	Dunn & Dunn
	Gregoric
	4Mat
	Silver/Strong/
	Hanson
	
	• **Multiple Intelligences**
	
	Using observation checklists, inventories,logs and journals to become more aware of how one learns
		Pre-assessment
		• **Before:**
		Formal
		Written pre-test
		Journaling
		Surveys/Inventories
		Informal
		Squaring off
		Boxing
		Graffiti Facts
		
		• **During:**
		Formal
		Journaling/Portfolios
		Teacher-made tests
		Checklists/Rubrics
		Informal
		Thumb it
		Fist of five
		Face the fact
		
		• **After:**
		Formal
		Post test
		Portfolio/Conferences
		Reflections
		Informal
		Talking Topics
		Conversation
		Circles
		Donut
			Adjustable Assignment
			
			Compacting
			
			T. A. P. S.
			Total Group
			Lecturette
			Presentation
			Demonstration
			Jigsaw
			Video
			Field Trip
			Guest Speaker
			Text
			
			Alone:
			• Interest
			• Personalized
			• Multiple
			  Intelligences
			Paired:
			• Random
			• Interest
			• Task
			Small Groups:
			• Heterogeneous
			• Homogeneous
			• Task Oriented
			• Constructed
			• Random
			• Interest
				• **Brain / Research Based**
				Memory model
				Elaborative rehearsal
				
				• Focus activities
				
				• Graphic organizers
				Compare & contrast
				Webbing
				
				• Metaphors
				
				• Cooperative group
				  learning
				
				• Jigsaw
				
				• Role play
					Centers
					
					Projects
					
					Problem Based
					
					Inquiry
					
					Contracts

SOURCE: Gayle H. Gregory and Carolyn Chapman, *Differentiated Instructional Strategies: One Size Doesn't Fit All*. Thousand Oaks, CA: Corwin Press, © 2002. Reproduction authorized only for the local school site that has purchased this book. www.corwinpress.com.

Figure 19   Differentiated instruction means keeping many balls in the air at once

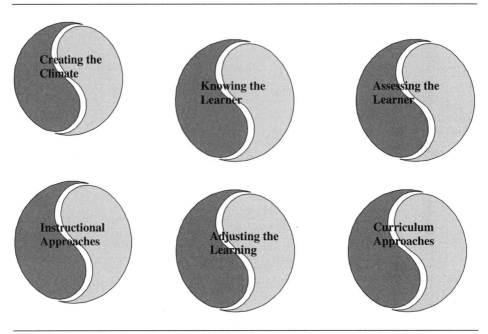

which differentiated instruction can flourish, there are multiple elements that we need to explore and be conscious of in our planning and teaching. Ask teachers to examine the framework and identify what they are already using in the classroom and why these elements are necessary to support differentiation.

It is important for teachers to realize that this is not a linear model. Rather, all the elements are essential, and we need to work continually on some or all of them, keeping many balls in the air at once (Figure 19).

Teachers may want to put green dots on familiar, already used strategies or techniques, and to highlight with yellow the ones that they would like to know more about. They may also want to identify one area that interests them, set a realistic goal for implementation, create some beginning steps, and set a timeline. A differentiation journal or a double-duty log (see Figure 11 in Chapter I-2) may be started at this time to facilitate reflection and to begin a chronicle of the journey into differentiation.

Figure 20   The Six-Step Planning Model for differentiated learning

PLANNING FOR DIFFERENTIATED LEARNING

1. STANDARDS: What should students know and be able to do?	Assessment tools for data collection: (logs, checklists, journals, agendas, observations, portfolios, rubrics, contracts)

Essential Questions:

2. CONTENT: (concepts, vocabulary, facts)	SKILLS:	

3. ACTIVATE: Focus Activity: Pre-assessment strategy Preassessment Prior knowledge & engaging the learners	• Quiz, test • Surveys • K.W.L. • Journals • Arm Gauge • Give me 5 • Brainstorm • Concept Formation • Thumb it
4. ACQUIRE: Total group or small groups	• Lecturette • Presentation • Demonstration • Jigsaw • Video • Field Trip • Guest Speaker • Text

Grouping Decisions: (T.A.P.S. random, heterogeneous, homogeneous, interest, task, constructed)

5. APPLY ADJUST			• Learning Centers • Projects • Contracts • Compact/Enrichment • Problem Based • Inquiry • Research • Independent study

6. ASSESS Diversity Honored (Learning Styles, Multiple Intelligences, personal interest etc)	• Quiz, test, • Performance • Products • Presentation • Demonstration • Log, journal, • Checklist • Portfolio • Rubric • Metacognition)

Using the Six-Step Planning Model for Differentiation

Present the Six-Step Planning Model (Figure 20). Discuss the designing down process and the six steps in planning:

1. Set standards.

2. Define content.

3. Activate prior knowledge.

4. Acquire new knowledge.

5. Apply and adjust the learning.

6. Assess the learning.

Chapter II-1

Creating a Climate for Learning

This chapter covers the fundamental elements that all learners need in order to succeed and to feel positive about their experiences in school. Strategies are based on *Differentiated Instructional Strategies: One Size Doesn't Fit All* (Gregory & Chapman, 2002a; pp. 1–17); page numbers enclosed in parentheses throughout this chapter refer to that book.

WHAT DO LEARNERS NEED TO SUCCEED? (PAGES 1–4)

Concept Formation (Taba, 1962, 1999)

1. Ask teachers to use self-sticking notes and brainstorm conditions conducive to learning, one idea per note.

2. Ask teachers to share their ideas in small groups and organize the suggestions written on their self-sticking notes according to like attributes.

3. When they have the notes organized by like attributes, ask the teachers to label each of the groupings.

Some teachers use the acronym **GROUP** to remember the steps:

G enerate

R e-examine

O rganize by similarities

U se a label to identify group

P rocess and discuss

Emotions and Learning (Pages 5–7)

1. Invite teachers to compare their ideas with Maslow (1954, 1968), Glasser (1990), and Kohn (1993).

2. Ask teachers to think of something they remember from high school and share it with a colleague. Have them discuss the emotions evoked, which are usually very positive or negative in nature. Emotions have a major impact on facilitating or inhibiting learning.

3. Show the video clip on climate from *Differentiating Instruction to Meet the Needs of All Learners.* Use the elementary tape (Gregory & Chapman, 2002b) at the 9-minute mark or the secondary tape (Gregory & Chapman, 2002c) at the 8:30 mark.

4. After showing the tape, ask teachers to generate strategies to set a classroom tone of acceptance and support.

Emotional Intelligence (Pages 7–8)

1. In small groups, have teachers read and discuss the five domains of Daniel Goleman's emotional intelligence (Goleman 1995, 1998).

2. Set up a Round the Room Brainstorming activity (Figure 21), giving each group a chart with one of the five domains (Figure 22).

3. One group at each chart will brainstorm ways to foster this competency in classrooms and then, at a signal, move on to the next chart. There they will read what the previous group wrote and will add more suggestions. At the signal they will move again until every group has attended each chart.

This strategy is an excellent one for collegial problem solving and generating ideas, thus fostering the learning community. It can also be used with the framework for the six elements of differentiation (Figure 18 in the Introduction to Part II), with one group working on a chart for each element to generate what teachers are already doing in each area.

Figure 21   Round the Room Brainstorming

1. Divide into groups, one group for each chart.

2. Each group should stand in front of a chart.

3. Choose a writer for each group.

4. Quickly brainstorm responses to the topic on the chart.

5. After a minute or two, and at the signal, move one chart to your right.

6. Quickly brainstorm at the new chart (2 minutes).

7. At the signal, move to the right and repeat.

8. When you reach the last chart, go back to the original chart to analyze the data. Select and/or prioritize, cluster, or eliminate.

Figure 22   Five domains of emotional intelligence

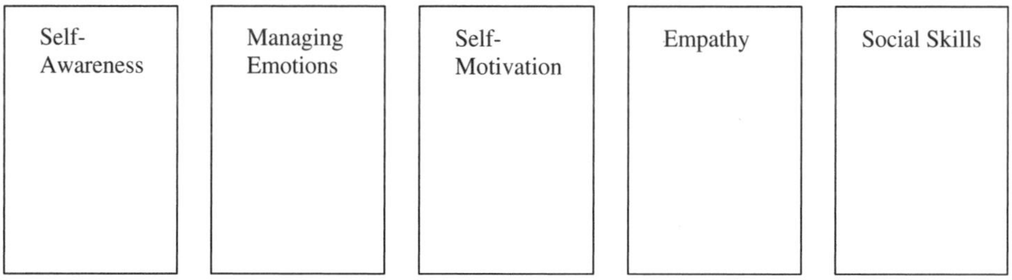

Self-Awareness	Managing Emotions	Self-Motivation	Empathy	Social Skills

Figure 23a   Question starters and classroom activities differentiated according to Bloom's taxonomy

QUESTION STARTERS

Level I: KNOWLEDGE (Recall)

1. What is the definition for . . . ?
2. What happened after . . . ?
3. Recall the facts.
4. What were the characteristics of . . . ?
5. Which is true or false?
6. How many . . . ?
7. Who was the . . . ?
8. Tell in your own words.

Level II: COMPREHENSION

1. Why are these ideas similar?
2. In your own words retell the story of . . .
3. What do you think could happen?
4. How are these ideas different?
5. Explain what happened after.
6. What are some examples?
7. Can you provide a definition of . . . ?
8. Who was the key character?

Level III: APPLICATION (applying without understanding is not effective)

1. What is another instance of . . . ?
2. Demonstrate the way to . . .
3. Which one is most like . . . ?
4. What questions would you ask?
5. Which factors would you change?
6. Could this have happened in . . . ? Why or why not?
7. How would you organize these ideas?

POTENTIAL ACTIVITIES

1. Describe the . . .
2. Make a time line of events
3. Make a facts chart
4. Write a list of . . . steps in . . . facts about . . .
5. List all the people in the story.
6. Make a chart showing . . .
7. Make an acrostic
8. Recite a poem.

1. Cut out or draw pictures to show an event.
2. Illustrate what you think the main idea was.
3. Make a cartoon strip showing the sequence of . . .
4. Write and perform a play based on the . . .
5. Compare this _____ with _____
6. Construct a model of . . .
7. Write a news report.
8. Prepare a flow chart to show the sequence . . .

1. Construct a model to demonstrate using it.
2. Make a display to illustrate one event.
3. Make a collection about . . .
4. Design a relief map to include relevant information about an event.
5. Scan a collection of photographs to illustrate a particular aspect of the study.
6. Create a mural to depict . . .

Figure 23b

QUESTION STARTERS	POTENTIAL ACTIVITIES
Level IV: **ANALYSIS** 1. What are the component parts of . . . ? 2. What steps are important in the process of . . . ? 3. If . . . then . . . 4. What other conclusions can you reach about . . . that have not been mentioned? 5. The difference between the fact and the hypothesis is . . . 6. The solution would be to . . . 7. What is the relationship between . . . and . . . ?	1. Design a questionnaire about . . . 2. Conduct an investigation to produce . . . 3. Make a flow chart to show . . . 4. Construct a graph to show . . . 5. Put on a play about . . . 6. Review . . . in terms of identified criteria. 7. Prepare a report about the area of study.
Level V: **SYNTHESIS** 1. Can you design a . . . ? 2. Why not compose a song about . . . ? 3. Why don't you devise your own way to . . . ? 4. Can you create new and unusual uses for . . . ? 5. Can you develop a proposal for . . . ? 6. How would you deal with . . . ? 7. Invent a scheme that would . . .	1. Create a model that shows your new ideas. 2. Devise an original plan or experiment for . . . 3. Finish the incomplete . . . 4. Make a hypothesis about . . . 5. Change . . . so that it will . . . 6. Propose a method to . . . 7. Prescribe a way to . . . 8. Give the book a new title.
Level VI: **EVALUATION** 1. In your opinion . . . 2. Appraise the chances for . . . 3. Grade or rank the . . . 4. What do you think should be the outcome? 5. What solution do you favor and why? 6. Which systems are best? Worst? 7. Rate the relative value of these ideas to . . . 8. Which is the better bargain?	1. Prepare a list of criteria you would use to judge a . . . Indicate priority ratings you would give. 2. Conduct a debate about an issue. 3. Prepare an annotated bibliography . . . 4. Form a discussion panel on the topic of . . . 5. Prepare a case to present your opinions about . . . 6. List some common assumptions about . . . Rationalize your reactions.

SOURCE: Gayle H. Gregory and Carolyn Chapman, *Differentiated Instructional Strategies: One Size Doesn't Fit All*. Thousand Oaks, CA: Corwin Press, © 2002. Reproduction authorized only for the local school site that has purchased this book. www.corwinpress.com

Instructional Technique: Questioning (Pages 8–9)

1. After reading the information about questioning (Gregory & Chapman, 2002a, pp. 8–9), have teachers discuss their experience with questioning and the strategies they already use to differentiate questioning.

2. Teachers who are interested in beginning to differentiate questioning may want to use the question starters displayed in Figure 23. Based on the different levels of Bloom's thinking taxonomy (Bloom et al., 1956), these two columns of question starters and potential activities may be printed on a colored piece of paper with the paper folded lengthwise and laminated. Teachers can then hold this as a prompt during total class discussions to give them language to use in differentiating questions to individuals in the class.

3. After using the question starters for some time in classes, teachers may want to discuss their successes or problems with questioning at a later meeting.

Instructional Technique: Cubing (Pages 9–15)

1. Have teachers read the information about cubing (Gregory & Chapman, 2002a, pp. 9–15) for another strategy that provides a variety of ways of examining an idea or concept. After the reading, have teachers discuss how cubing can be used in their classrooms.

2. Show the video *Differentiating Instruction: Tape 2* (Tomlinson, 1998b), focusing on the end of the tape, which covers interest surveys, flexible grouping, and cubing. Give teachers an advanced organizer

Figure 24   Advanced organizer for cubing lesson video

How did the teacher use interest surveys? What value did she see in them? What are your thoughts about interest surveys?	
How was flexible grouping used?	
What was differentiated in this lesson?	
What thinking skills were targeted? How were visual representations incorporated?	
What are your thoughts and ideas about the use of cubing?	

Figure 25   Rolling the dice

A. They describe it.

B. They compare it to a traditional instruction.

C. They associate it to other concepts.

D. They analyze the elements.

E. They apply it to their students.

F. They argue for or against it.

(Figure 24) to collect data and analyze their reactions to the classroom scenario.

3. After viewing the video, encourage teachers to share data recorded on their advanced organizers and discuss the uses of cubing in their classrooms.

4. Using large-sized store-bought dice, have teachers take turns in small groups rolling the dice and responding to the concept of differentiation in relationship to the number that they roll (Figure 25). The question starters in Figure 23 may be useful as prompts for their responses.

How Can We Use Cubes?

1. In a planning meeting, ask teachers to review the five steps for using cubes (Gregory & Chapman, 2002a, p. 12):

   - Keep clear learning goals in mind.
   - Provide extended opportunities and materials appropriate for a wide range of readiness, interests, and learning styles.
   - Make sure students understand the verbs and task directions.

Figure 26 Different verbs, tasks, and commands on each side of a cube show different levels of thinking

Cubing . . . Levels of Thinking	
1. Tell Describe Recall Name Locate List	**4. Review** Discuss Prepare Diagram Cartoon
2. Compare Contrast Example Explain Define Write	**5. Propose** Suggest Finish Prescribe Devise
3. Connect Make Design Produce Develop	**6. Debate** Formulate Choose Support In your opinion . . .

Reprinted from *Differentiated Instructional Strategies: One Size Doesn't Fit All*, by Gayle H. Gregory and Carolyn Chapman. Thousand Oaks, CA: Corwin Press, © 2002. www.corwinpress.com

- Group students according to readiness, understanding, and ability levels.
- Ask students to share findings with the larger group or to form expert groups.

2. Teachers can work in pairs or small groups using Figure 26 (levels of thinking) and Figure 27 (abilities and interests) to develop a

Figure 27 Cubes vary in color and task depending on the abilities and interests of the learners

Green Cube	Blue Cube
1.	1.
2.	2.
3.	3.
4.	4.
5.	5.
6.	6.
Yellow Cube	**Red Cube**
1.	1.
2.	2.
3.	3.
4.	4.
5.	5.
6.	6.

lesson or centers using cubing to differentiate instruction to meet the needs of students in their classrooms. They may also consider multiple intelligences (Gardner, 1983, 1993) in lesson planning.

Classroom Climate (Pages 15–17)

1. Have teachers read the information about classroom climate (Gregory & Chapman, 2002a, pp. 15–17).

2. After the reading, have teachers discuss how they create a positive physical and emotional climate.

3. Ask the teachers to experiment with different types of music to set a mood for the learning. An action research inquiry could be, How does music affect the learning and the learner?

Chapter II-2
Knowing
the Learner

This chapter looks at how students differ in their learning styles and intelligences. Page references in parentheses are from *Differentiated Instructional Strategies: One Size Doesn't Fit All* (Gregory & Chapman, 2002a).

LEARNING STYLES (PAGES 20–22)

1. After reading about the work of Dunn and Dunn and their five learning styles (Dunn & Dunn, 1987; Gregory & Chapman, 2002a, pp. 20–22), invite teachers to work in small groups using a round robin technique. Teachers will pass around a graphic organizer (Figure 28) to brainstorm the types of instructional and classroom practices each learning style would appreciate.

2. As teachers pass the graphic organizer around the table, each person will act in turn as the recorder for one quadrant. This can also be done on butcher paper so that all can see and so that the groups may post their charts.

3. DOVE rules for brainstorming (Figure 29) may also be used for this process. This is a useful acronym for people to examine during brainstorming as it reminds them of the attributes of brainstorming and that speed and numerous ideas are important.

4. Teachers may also consider using the survey "How Do You Like to Learn?" (Figure 30). Ask them how they might use the survey or modify it for their students.

Figure 28   Graphic organizer for five learning styles round robin

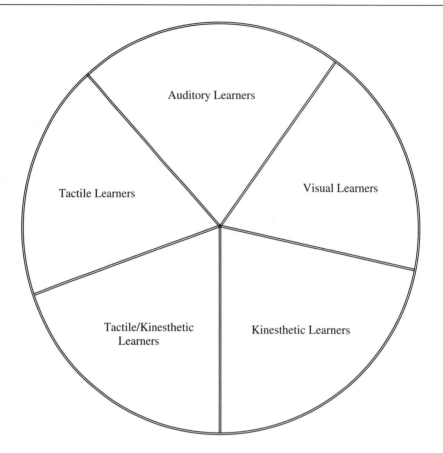

Figure 29   DOVE rules for brainstorming (adapted from Bennett, Rolheiser-Bennett, & Stevahn, 1991; and Bellanca & Fogarty, 1991)

D o accept all ideas

O pt for original thoughts

V ariety and volume

E xpand on others' ideas

Figure 30   How Do You Like to Learn?

1. Do you like music on while you study, or do you prefer a quiet place?
    Quiet   Music

2. Where would you prefer to work on an assignment?
    Classroom   Desk (home)
    On the floor   At a table
    On a computer

3. If you are not able to complete something, is it because
    You forgot?   It's boring?
    You got distracted?   You need help?

4. Where do like to sit in class?
    Near the door   Front
    By the wall   Near a window
    Back

5. Do you like to work with a partner?
    Why or why not?

6. Are you more alert in the afternoon?
    In the evening?
    In the morning?

7. What classes do you enjoy most and why?

    _____
    _____
    _____

8. Describe how you study. Where? When? How?

    _____
    _____
    _____

9. If you have an assignment due in two weeks, how do you plan to complete it?

    _____
    _____
    _____

10. If something is new for you, do you
    Like to have it explained?   Like to read about it?
    Like to watch a video/   Like to just try it?
       demonstration?

THINKING STYLES (PAGES 22–28)

1. Ask teachers to read the section on thinking styles (Gregory & Chapman, 2002a, pp. 22–24) based on the work of Gregorc (1982), Kolb (1984), and McCarthy (1990). Encourage a discussion about the similarities among the three theories.

2. Ask teachers to consider the four commonly known items of beach ball, microscope, puppy, and clipboard, and decide which one they think is most representative of themselves.

3. After teachers share their decisions and reasons for choosing their items, invite them to go to one of the four corners of the room to match the item they selected (Figure 31). Each corner can be labeled with one of the four items: beach ball, microscope, puppy, or clipboard.

4. Using a large sheet of paper, ask the teachers in each corner to brainstorm the attributes of this type of thinker and also the things that their type of learner would appreciate in the classroom. For example, puppies might say that they like people and would appreciate cooperative learning tasks.

5. Encourage the teachers to investigate learning styles further through reading additional resources and sharing their newfound information with others at another meeting.

Figure 31   Four corners activity for learning styles and thinking styles

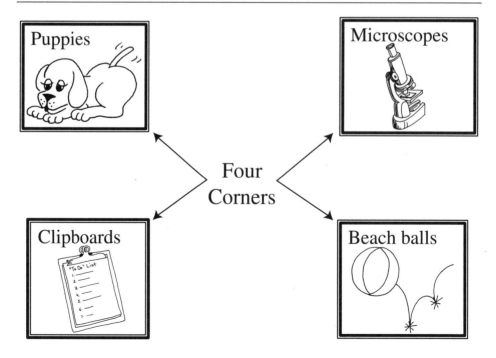

MULTIPLE INTELLIGENCES (PAGES 28–35)

1. After reading this section, ask teachers to speculate how they incorporate multiple intelligences in the classrooms.

2. Encourage teachers to begin with themselves and become more metacognitive about their own multiple intelligences. Using the "How Are You Intelligent?" chart (Figure 32), ask teachers to check off the statements that most represent them.

3. Photocopy the "What Is Your Unique Multiple Intelligences Profile?" chart (Figure 33) on a variety of colored sheets of 8.5-by-11-inch paper.

4. Ask the teachers to create their profiles by transferring the number of items that they checked in each category of Figure 32 to the

Figure 32   How Are You Intelligent?

VERBAL/LINGUISTIC INTELLIGENCE	INTRAPERSONAL INTELLIGENCE
• I like to tell jokes, tell stories or tales. • Books are important to me. • I like to read. • I often listen to radio, TV, tapes, or CDs. • I write easily and enjoy it. • I quote things I've read. • I like crosswords and word games.	• I know about my feelings, strengths, and weaknesses. • I like to learn more about myself. • I enjoy hobbies by myself. • I enjoy being alone sometimes. • I have confidence in myself. • I like to work alone. • I think about things and plan what to do next.
LOGICAL/MATHEMATICAL INTELLIGENCE	**VISUAL/SPATIAL INTELLIGENCE**
• I solve math problems easily. • I enjoy math and using computers. • I like strategy games. • I wonder how things work. • I like using logic to solve problems. • I reason things out. • I like to use data in my work to measure, calculate, and analyze.	• I shut my eyes and see clear pictures. • I think in pictures. • I like color and interesting designs. • I can find my way around unfamiliar areas. • I draw and doodle. • I like books with pictures, maps, and charts. • I like videos, movies, and photographs.
INTERPERSONAL INTELLIGENCE	**BODILY/KINESTHETIC INTELLIGENCE**
• People ask me for advice. • I prefer team sports. • I have many close friends. • I like working in groups. • I'm comfortable in a crowd. • I have empathy for others. • I can figure out what people are feeling.	• I get uncomfortable when I sit too long. • I like to touch or be touched when talking. • I use my hand when speaking. • I like working with my hands on crafts/hobbies. • I touch things to learn more about them. • I think of myself as well coordinated. • I learn by doing rather than watching.
MUSICAL/RHYTHMIC INTELLIGENCE	**NATURALIST**
• I like to listen to musical selections. • I am sensitive to music and sounds. • I can remember tunes. • I listen to music when studying. • I enjoy singing. • I keep time to music. • I have a good sense of rhythm.	• I enjoy spending time in nature. • I like to classify things into categories. • I can hear animal and bird sounds clearly. • I see details when I look at plants, flowers, and trees. • I am happiest out doors. • I like tending to plants and animals. • I know the names of trees, plants, birds, and animals.

SOURCE: Gayle H. Gregory and Carolyn Chapman, *Differentiated Instructional Strategies: One Size Doesn't Fit All*. Thousand Oaks, CA: Corwin Press, © 2002. Reproduction authorized only for the local school site that has purchased this book. www.corwinpress.com

Figure 33   What Is Your Unique Multiple Intelligences Profile?

Word Smart							
Math Smart							
People Smart							
Music Smart							
Self Smart							
Picture Smart							
Body Smart							
Nature							

SOURCE: Adapted by permission of SkyLight Professional Development from page 57 of *Integrating Curricula with Multiple Intelligences: Teams, Themes, and Threads* by Robin Fogarty and Judy Stoehr. © 1995 IRI/SkyLight Training and Publishing, Inc. www.skylightedu.com

relevant spot in Figure 33. After they finish, invite them to compare their profiles with other staff members to examine the differences in their strengths and areas of need.

5. Invite teachers to share how they get to know their students and also to examine Figures 34, 35, and 36 to see how they might use them for data collection and student awareness and reflection.

Figure 34   Teachers can capture observations over time about students' multiple intelligences and transfer them to student profiles

---

STUDENT PROFILE

Observing over time . . .   Name:

Verbal/Linguistic	Intrapersonal
Logical/Mathematical	Visual/Spacial
Interpersonal	Bodily/Kinesthetic
Musical/Rhythmic	Naturalist

SOURCE: Gayle H. Gregory and Carolyn Chapman, *Differentiated Instructional Strategies: One Size Doesn't Fit All*. Thousand Oaks, CA: Corwin Press, © 2002. Reproduction authorized only for the local school site that has purchased this book. www.corwinpress.com

6. Another suggestion is to photocopy and laminate Figure 37 and use it when planning to spark ideas that may help teachers vary instruction and assessment and give students a choice in how they learn and show what they know.

Figure 35   Eight intelligences: Self-reflection tool to use individually or with peers

Complete this page and compare your answers with your partner.

If I could do anything I like, I'd . . . .

Usually, when I have free time I . . . .

My hobbies are . . . .

At school I like to . . . .

The type of things that we do in class I really like are . . . .

I am uncomfortable when people ask me to . . . .

Do you like to work alone or with a group? Why?

SOURCE: Gayle H. Gregory and Carolyn Chapman, *Differentiated Instructional Strategies: One Size Doesn't Fit All.* Thousand Oaks, CA: Corwin Press, © 2002. Reproduction authorized only for the local school site that has purchased this book. www.corwinpress.com

7. Show the video *Differentiating Instruction to Meet the Needs of All Learners,* secondary edition, Tape 2, at the 34-minute point (Gregory & Chapman, 2002c). This section shows a secondary consumer science teacher who uses the inventory to help students assess their strengths and then offers them a choice in their assignment by selecting a project from a list of suggestions (see Gregory & Chapman, 2002a, pp. 122–123 for a sample list).

Figure 36 Yes-Maybe-No list

1.
2.
3.
4.
5.
6.
7.
8.
9.
10.

Ask students about a variety of activities that they might have the opportunity to do.

How do you feel about . . .

1. Drawing and artwork?
2. Musical activities?
3. Working with others?
4. Working alone?
5. Using numbers?
6. Writing? Talking?
7. Dancing, sports, moving while learning?
8. Solving problems?
9. Reading?
10. Thinking about things?
11. Working with technology?
12. Being a leader?

Figure 37   Suggestions for using the eight multiple intelligences

MUSICAL RHYTHMIC

Sing it
Create a beat
Rap it
Make a cheer
Create a jingle
Hum it
Identify sounds
React to sounds
Listen to sounds
Connect to music
Write a poem

VERBAL LINGUISTIC

Read it
Spell it
Write it
Listen to it
Tell it
Recall it
Use "you" words
Apply it
Chunk information
Say it
Discuss it
Use mnemonics

LOGICAL MATHEMATICAL

Make a pattern
Chart it
Sequence it
Create a mnemonic
Analyze it
Think abstractly
Think critically
Use numbers
Prove it
Interpret the data
Use the statistics

VISUAL SPATIAL

Mind maps
Graphic organizers
Video
Color code
Highlight
Shape a word
Interpret a graphic
Read a chart
Study illustrations
Visualize it
Make a chart
Create a poster

Multiple Intelligences
"Making Learning Palatable"

BODY KINESTHETIC

Role play
Walkabout
Dance
Lip sync
Skits/charades/mime
Construction
Math manipulatives
Sign language
Sports
Activity centers
Body language

INTRAPERSONAL

Metacognition
Use self-talk
Work independently
Solve it your own way
Understand self
Journal it
Rehearse it
Use prior knowledge
Connect it
Have ownership

INTERPERSONAL

Think-Pair-Share
Jigsaw
Cooperative grouping
Drama
Debates
Class meetings
Role play
Meeting of minds
Peer counseling
Tutors/buddies
Shared journals
Giving feedback

NATURALIST

Label it
Categorize it
Identify it
Form a hypothesis
Do an experiment
Adapt it
Construct it
Classify it
Investigate it
Discern patterns

SOURCE: Adapted from *Test Success in the Brain Compatible Classroom* (Chapman & King, 2000) and from presentation materials by Gayle Gregory (1998)

8. Invite teachers to examine the choices in Figure 38 and consider how they might offer students choices in the areas of multiple intelligences.

Figure 38 Multiple intelligences: Suggestions for centers and projects

Verbal/Linguistic
Prepare a report
Write a play or essay
Create a poem or recitation
Listen to an audiotape on . . .
Interview
Label a diagram
Give directions for . . .

Bodily/Kinesthetic
Create a role-play
Construct a model
        or representation
Develop a mime
Create a tableau for . . .
Manipulate materials
Work through a simulation
Create actions for . . .

Musical/Rhythmic
Compose a rap song or rhyme
Create a jingle to teach others . . .
Listen to musical selections about . . .
Write a poem
Select music or songs
        for a particular purpose

Interpersonal
Work with a partner or group
Discuss and come
        to conclusions
Solve a problem together
Survey or interview others
Dialogue about a topic
Use cooperative groups

Naturalist
Discover or experiment
Categorize materials or ideas
Look for ideas from nature
Adapt materials to a new use
Connect ideas to nature
Examine materials
        to make generalizations

Logical/Mathematical
Create a pattern
Describe a sequence or process
Develop a rationale
Analyze a situation
Critically assess . . .
Classify, rank, or compare . . .
Interpret evidence . . .

Visual/Spatial
Draw a picture
Create a mural or display
Illustrate an event
Make a diagram
Create a cartoon
Paint or design a poster
Design a graphic
Use color to . . .

Intrapersonal
Think about and plan
Write in a journal
Review or visualize a way
        to do something
Make a connection with
        past information or experiences
Metacognitive moments

SOURCE: Gayle H. Gregory and Carolyn Chapman, *Differentiated Instructional Strategies: One Size Doesn't Fit All.* Thousand Oaks, CA: Corwin Press, © 2002. Reproduction authorized only for the local school site that has purchased this book. www.corwinpress.com

Figure 39   Brainstorming multiple intelligence choices

Standards:_____

Content:_____

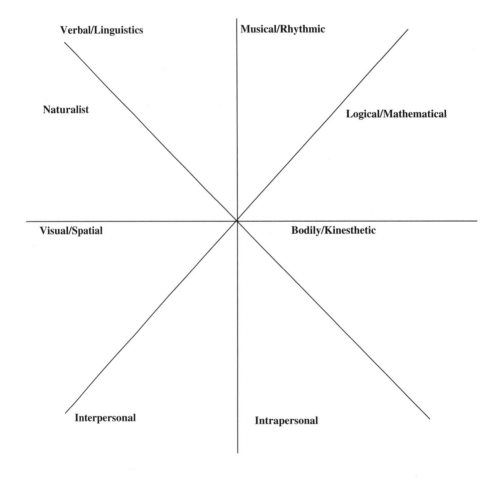

Figure 40   Contract form student fills in after choosing an activity

Name_____ Unit of study_____

I agree to complete the following activity: _____

I chose this option because_____

Please outline your plan: _____

_____

By the (date)_____
Signature_____

9. Teachers may also want to select a topic and standards that they plan to teach in the near future. Using the organizer in Figure 39, they can fill in the topic and learning goals targeted. Then, with a partner, they can brainstorm possibilities for learning and assessment in the eight intelligences that could be used in the classroom. After the brainstorming, teachers may examine and critically select those that they think would be most effective for the students with whom they are working.

10. Teachers also may want to consider setting up a contract system using some of these options (see Figures 40 and 41).

Figure 41   Contract form on which the teacher recommends core activities

Author Study Contract

To help you improve your reading and writing you will complete the core activities and may choose any optional activities that total at least 40 points.

Please fill in the contract and hand it in by _____ .

Core Activities that everyone will do: (Points)

1. I will select and begin a book by _____ . (5)

2. I will create a "mindmap" character sketch about a main character in my book, (appearance, personality, friends/family, likes/dislikes). (10)

3. Each author uses languages in interesting ways. Select 3 passages that you think are unique and explain in your own words their meaning and why you think the author expressed himself or herself in this way. (10)

Optional selections:

4. I will write a dialogue that I could role-play about a situation or problem that I read. 1 page (10)

5. I will draw a story map or comic strip with captions outlining the plot. (10)

6. I will write a commercial, design a poster, or produce a brochure on the computer to advertise my book and/or the author. (5)

7. As a critic I will write an article sharing my thoughts about the story, outlining what I thought was Plus, Minus, and Interesting (De Bono). This will be a full page column. I will use the word processing program on the computer. (10)

8. Design an option and discuss with the teacher. (5 or 10)

This will give me _____ points.

Signed by Student _____

Signed by Teacher _____

Chapter II-3

Assessing the Learner

The Big Question this chapter asks is, How does or should differentiated instruction impact assessment and evaluation? (Page references in parentheses are from *Differentiated Instructional Strategies: One Size Doesn't Fit All* by Gayle Gregory and Carolyn Chapman, 2002a.)

DEFINITIONS (PAGE 37)

1. To start, invite teachers to write in their own words definitions for the terms *assessment, evaluation,* and *grading* (Figure 42).

2. After teachers have written their own definitions, ask them to compare their definitions with those of Rolheiser, Bower, and Stevahn (2000) and with the discussion of assessment in *Differentiated*

Figure 42   Defining assessment and evaluation

Assessment means …
Evaluation means …
Grading means …

Figure 43   The merits of pre-assessment

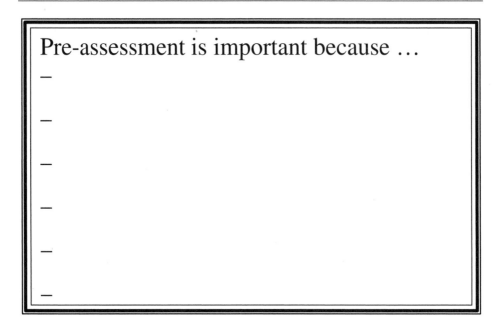

> Pre-assessment is important because …
>
> –
>
> –
>
> –
>
> –
>
> –
>
> –

Instructional Strategies: One Size Doesn't Fit All (Gregory & Chapman, 2002a, p. 37).

PURPOSES OF PRE-ASSESSMENT (PAGES 38–40)

1. As a group, ask teachers to list and discuss the merits of pre-assessing students (Figure 43).

2. Facilitate a dialogue focusing on all the positive reasons they've listed.

3. Move the discussion to the important follow-up question: With all those positive reasons for pre-assessing students, why isn't pre-assessment more widely practiced?

PRE-ASSESSMENTS (PAGES 40–42)

1. Show the pre-assessment section from one of the videos on *Differentiating Instruction to Meet the Needs of All Learners.* If you use the elementary edition (Gregory & Chapman, 2002b), show Tape 1, 21 minutes (section on pre-assessment and assessment) and/or 4–11:30 minutes (pre-assessment). If you use the secondary edition (Gregory & Chapman, 2002c), show Tape 2 on pre-assessment using mind maps at the 4-minute mark.

2. Ask teachers to list the pre-assessment techniques shown in the video they have just seen.

3. Review the pre-assessment strategies in the book (Gregory & Chapman, 2002a, pp. 40–42).

4. Ask teachers to list the pre-assessment techniques covered in the book.

ASSESSMENT TOOLS TO USE BEFORE, DURING, AND AFTER LEARNING (PAGES 40–48)

1. Ask teachers to select a partner for this activity, which will involve looking at several types of informal pre-assessment before, during, and after each lesson.

2. Assign the activities to the partners, choosing from the following selection:

Pre-assessment (Pages 40–42)

- Squaring Off
- Boxing
- Yes/No Cards
- Graffiti Facts

During the Learning (Pages 42–44)

- Thumb It
- Fist of Five
- Face the Fact
- Reaching for the Top
- Speedometer Reading

After the Learning (Pages 44–47)

- Wraparounds
- Talking Topics
- Conversation Circles
- Donut
- Rotation Reflection
- Paper Pass
- Grand Finale Comments

3. With their partners, teachers will demonstrate one of the informal assessments to the group and suggest when they might use it.

Figure 44a   Sample interest survey questions

Sample Interest Survey Questions

	Rarely Ever	Sometimes	Most of the Time
1. I like to make up songs.			
2. I like to try things that are hard to do.			
3. Brain puzzles hold my interest.			
4. I like to take things apart and assemble them.			
5. I enjoy creating.			
6. I need manipulatives to learn.			
7. I am a follower.			
8. I am a leader.			
9. I prefer to work alone.			
10. I like to read.			
11. I prefer to work with others.			
12. I like to draw my own pictures.			
13. I can see visual images in my head.			
14. I have at least one pet.			
15. I enjoy animals.			
16. I would rather be outside than inside.			
17. I would rather be inside than outside.			
18. I like school.			
19. I do not like school.			
20. School would be better if _____.			

Figure 44b

21. If I have free time I prefer to

    a. _____

    b. _____

    c. _____

22. I do not like _____ because _____.

23. Additional Comments

    a. _____

    b. _____

Sample Unit Interest Survey

Focus: Study of a country

□ History

□ Industry

□ Beliefs

□ Government

□ Celebrations, festivals, holidays, and rites

□ Geography and location

SURVEYS (PAGES 47–49)

1. Review the sample interest survey questions (Figure 44) and discuss the usefulness of surveys.

2. Ask the teachers to think about a survey that they might use for an upcoming unit of study. This survey may uncover interests as well as how students may want to learn the lesson content and with whom they may wish to work.

ONGOING ASSESSMENT AND PORTFOLIOS (PAGES 49–51)

1. Encourage teachers to discuss portfolios as a method of assessing student learning. What are the advantages? Issues? Concerns?

2. Encourage teachers who are already using student portfolios to serve as valuable resources that other staff members may access for information, processes, and reflection tools.

3. Suggest other resources that teachers can use for student portfolios. Consider using *The Portfolio Organizer* (Rolheiser et al., 2000) or *Portfolios Across the Curriculum and Beyond* (Cole, Ryan, Kick, & Mathies, 2000).

GRADING (PAGES 52–53)

Another issue that concerns teachers who are moving toward more differentiated classrooms is grading. Organize a discussion around the following questions:

1. What is grading?

2. What is the purpose of grading?

3. How is our school's or system's grading process helpful to learning?

4. What might change as we differentiate instruction and assessment?

AUTHENTIC TASKS (PAGES 53–55)

Review the list of authentic tasks in Figure 45. Organize a discussion around the following questions:

1. What is critical in planning so that these activities are not just fun and engaging but offer students experiences that provide real learning?

2. How could these activities be differentiated further based on students' readiness, interest, level of independence, or learning styles?

3. Thinking about giving students a choice, what might be done to offer choices with realistic expectations for different students?

Figure 45   Authentic assessment activities

Make a mural

Plan a trip

Conduct a panel

Create a magazine

Develop a display

Create a talk show

Choreograph a dance

Create costumes

Draw a comic strip

Teach a lesson

Create a flow chart

Design a video

Complete a portfolio

Write lyrics for a song

Design a survey and interview

Conduct a demonstration

Illustrate a story

Create a puppet play

Design a bulletin board

Create a timeline on the computer

Role-play the story

Write a persuasive article

Develop a new innovation to . . . .

Reprinted from *Differentiated Instructional Strategies: One Size Doesn't Fit All*, by Gayle H. Gregory and Carolyn Chapman. Thousand Oaks, CA: Corwin Press, © 2002. www.corwinpress.com

Chapter II-4

Adjusting, Compacting, and Grouping

ADJUSTABLE ASSIGNMENTS (PAGES 58–63)

1. Ask teachers to define what we mean by *adjustable assignments*.

2. Challenge teachers to come up with an analogy for an adjustable assignment.

3. Use the Slinky analogy for an adjustable assignment (Figure 46). Ask teachers to list all the reasons why an adjustable assignment is like a Slinky.

4. Create a symbol that supports the Slinky analogy.

5. Screen the adjustable assignments section of the video *Differentiating Instruction to Meet the Needs of All Learners,* secondary edition, Tape 2, at the 13-minute mark (Gregory & Chapman, 2002c).

6. Invite teachers to review the adjustable assignments section of the text *Differentiated Instructional Strategies: One Size Doesn't Fit All* (Gregory & Chapman, 2002a, pp. 58–62) and to examine Figures 47 and 48 following.

Figure 46 Slinky analogy for adjustable assignments

An adjustable assignment is like a Slinky because_____
_____
_____
_____
_____
_____
_____
_____
_____. Create a symbol.

Figure 47 Sample adjustable assignment: Money

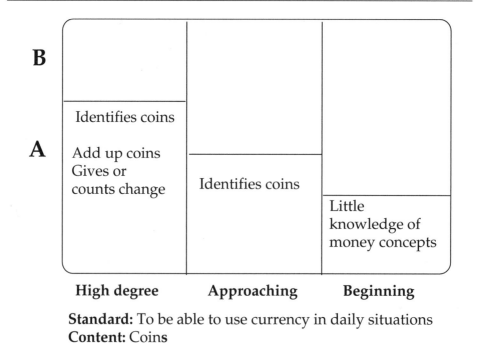

Standard: To be able to use currency in daily situations
Content: Coins

Figure 48   Sample adjustable assignment: Spanish

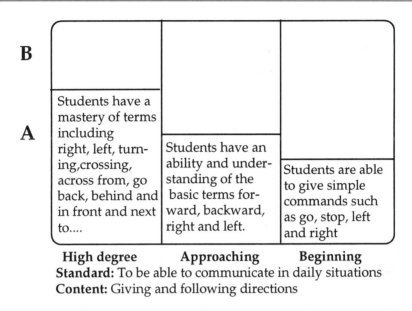

B

A

| Students have a mastery of terms including right, left, turning, crossing, across from, go back, behind and in front and next to.... | Students have an ability and understanding of the basic terms forward, backward, right and left. | Students are able to give simple commands such as go, stop, left and right |

High degree   **Approaching**   **Beginning**

Standard: To be able to communicate in daily situations
Content: Giving and following directions

Adjusting Assignments

1. Ask teachers to form pairs or grade-level groups to create a chart on butcher paper as shown in Figure 49.

2. Suggest that teachers identify a standard or learning outcome and a topic or content to be studied.

3. Their next step is to identify a method of pre-assessing their students. Considering the standard or skill to be targeted:

   • What would be an appropriate pre-assessment technique?
   • Would an interest survey be applicable?
   • What formal or informal strategies could be used?

4. Teachers may then predict what learners may know or can do at perhaps three levels and log this information on the Figure 49 chart in Section A.

5. Considering the data, what might be offered as a learning experience for students at the beginning level, the approaching level, and the high degree of competencies?

Figure 49 Adjustable assignment grid for recording data about student readiness levels

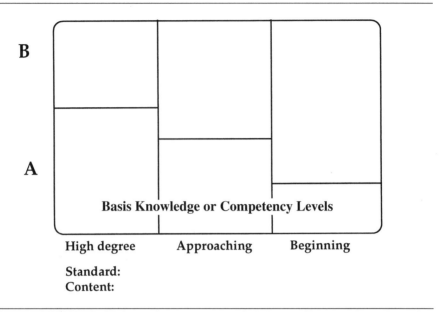

Reprinted from *Differentiated Instructional Strategies: One Size Doesn't Fit All*, by Gayle H. Gregory and Carolyn Chapman. Thousand Oaks, CA: Corwin Press, © 2002. www.corwinpress.com

6. Encourage teachers to follow the process in their classroom and experiment with the pre-assessment strategies and their instructional decisions based on the pre-assessment data.

Adjustable Review

1. At the next meeting, encourage teachers to share the outcomes of their experimentation through the examination of student work and reflection on their decisions.

2. Screen the video *Differentiating Instruction to Meet the Needs of All Learners*, elementary edition, Tape 2, at the 132-minute mark, "Adjustable Review with Ellen Wilken," grade 7 math teacher (Gregory & Chapman, 2002b).

3. Discuss how differentiating learning and respecting students is evident in this clip.

Figure 50   Upside, downside, on side

Upside What are the positives for compacting? 	
Downside What are the negatives associated with compacting? 	
On side What have I already done related to compacting? 	

CURRICULUM COMPACTING (PAGES 63–66)

1. Invite teachers to review the curriculum compacting section of the text *Differentiated Instructional Strategies: One Size Doesn't Fit All* (Gregory & Chapman, 2002a, pp. 63–66).

2. Facilitate a discussion focusing on the following questions:
   - What is compacting?
   - Why do we use it?
   - How do we do it?

3. Introduce the tactic Upside, Downside, On side (Figure 50).

Figure 51   Collaborative jigsaw compacting

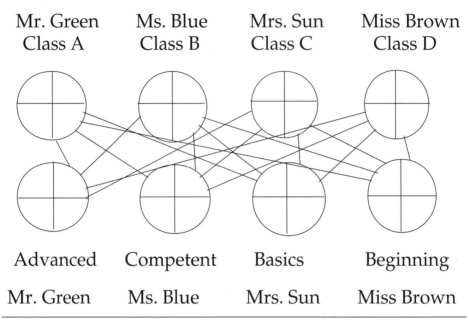

Mr. Green Class A	Ms. Blue Class B	Mrs. Sun Class C	Miss Brown Class D

Advanced	Competent	Basics	Beginning
Mr. Green	Ms. Blue	Mrs. Sun	Miss Brown

Reprinted from *Differentiated Instructional Strategies: One Size Doesn't Fit All*, by Gayle H. Gregory and Carolyn Chapman. Thousand Oaks, CA: Corwin Press, © 2002. www.corwinpress.com

COLLABORATIVE PLANNING MODELS FOR COMPACTING (PAGES 66–70)

1. Ask teachers to consider the planning models for compacting in the Gregory and Chapman (2002a) text.

2. Introduce Figure 51 on collaborative jigsaw compacting.

3. Ask the teachers to discuss which models they might investigate further for use in their own classrooms:

   • Would this be a model that is feasible in our school?
   • How might that work?
   • Which teachers might work together?

FLEXIBLE GROUPING (PAGES 70–78)

1. Take a few minutes to think about and discuss why and how students are grouped.

2. Consider TAPS (Figure 52) and the types of grouping that teachers use. Use Figure 53 to list when and how each type of group might be used.

Figure 52 TAPS

Total Group
Alone
Partner
Small Group

TAPS (a rap)

Remember!

Some things need to be taught to the class as a whole.
There are certain things the Total Group should be told.

Working Alone, students get to problem-solve in their own way.
They will be in charge of what they think, do, and say.

With a Partner, many thoughts and ideas they can share.
They can work and show each other the solutions there.

Effective Small Groups work together to cooperate
Using the group's ideas and talents their learning
will accelerate.

So use a variety of ways to group students you see.
This TAPS into student's potential, as it should be.

Reprinted from *Differentiated Instructional Strategies: One Size Doesn't Fit All*, by Gayle H. Gregory and Carolyn Chapman. Thousand Oaks, CA: Corwin Press, © 2002. www.corwinpress.com

3. Invite teachers to work in pairs to create wallpaper posters (Figure 54) examining and clarifying one of the following small group designs. (All topics listed are from Gregory and Chapman, *Differentiated Instructional Strategies: One Size Doesn't Fit All*, 2002a. Page numbers refer to that volume.) These charts may be presented and discussed with colleagues.

   A. Knowledge of a Subject (p. 72)
   B. Ability to Perform a Task or a Skill (p. 72)

Figure 53   Using each type of group

Grouping Type	Used for
Total Group	
Alone	
Paired	
Small groups	

C. Interests in a Specific Area of the Content (p. 73)
D. Peer-to-Peer Tutoring (p. 73)
E. Cooperative Learning (pp. 74–77)
F. Sharing Groups (p. 74)

Figure 54 Wallpaper poster clarifying small group design

Wallpaper Poster

• Define it!

• Draw a symbol to represent it!

• Give an example of its use!

- Energizing Partners
- Brainstorming Bash
- Total Class Brainstorming Bash
- Adjustable Assignment Brainstorming Bash
- Community Clusters
- Content Talk
- Research Probes
- Experiment, Lab, Center, Station, or Project Groups

G. Multiage Grouping (p. 77)

Grouping Aids

1. Often "make and take" sessions may be held during lunchtime or in a short before-school meeting to actually construct things that would make life easier in the classroom.

2. Ask teachers to share ways of randomly grouping students. Provide time to construct "wagon wheel" teaming (Figure 55), based on the idea developed by Sheila Silversides (in Kagan, 1992) for mixed ability groups, learning styles (beach balls, clipboards, puppies, microscopes), or using student strengths in the multiple intelligences.

3. As an alternate or additional activity, teachers may use craft sticks or tongue depressors to create random groupings using the technique described in Figure 56.

Figure 55   Wagon Wheel Teaming: Rotating concentric circles to form teams of three or four learners at different levels

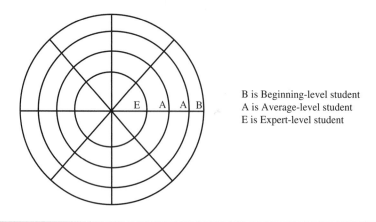

B is Beginning-level student
A is Average-level student
E is Expert-level student

Figure 56   Stick Picks: Used to create random groups of heterogeneous learners

Number	Color	Color	Number	Color	Color
1	blue	orange	19	yellow	orange
2	yellow	pink	20	green	purple
3	red	purple	21	red	pink
4	green	pink	22	blue	purple
5	yellow	orange	23	green	orange
6	blue	purple	24	yellow	pink
7	green	purple	25	blue	pink
8	red	pink	26	green	purple
9	red	orange	27	red	orange
10	green	orange	28	yellow	orange
11	blue	pink	29	yellow	pink
12	yellow	purple	30	green	purple
13	yellow	purple	31	blue	orange
14	red	orange	32	red	pink
15	green	pink	33	red	purple
16	blue	pink	34	yellow	purple
17	blue	purple	35	blue	pink
18	red	orange	36	green	orange

Chapter II-5

Instructional Strategies for Student Success

RATIONALE FOR UNDERSTANDING
HOW THE BRAIN WORKS (PAGES 79–84)

1. Present the following question for teachers to consider and discuss: If we can drive a car and not understand how engines operate, and if we can use a VCR and not know how to program it, why is it important to know about the brain?

2. In order to examine what we know about how the brain processes information, ask teachers to consider the following aspects of the process.

   - Memory
   - Context
   - Associating concepts
   - Attention
   - Rehearsal
   - Emotions
   - Recall and rehearsal

3. Using the same jigsaw strategy that also worked in Chapter I-2, refer to Figure 57. To facilitate the process, ask each person, pair, or small group to select one aspect of the process and read, interpret, and teach the others about the concept by applying it to their experience in the classroom.

Figure 57 Jigsaw strategy for advanced learners

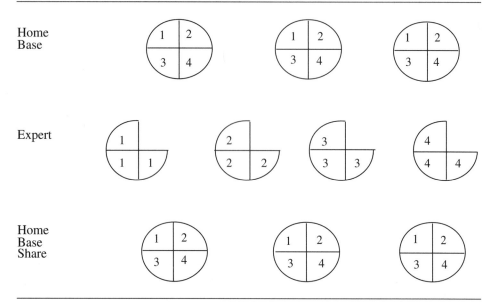

Reprinted from *Differentiated Instructional Strategies: One Size Doesn't Fit All*, by Gayle H. Gregory and Carolyn Chapman. Thousand Oaks, CA: Corwin Press, © 2002. www.corwinpress.com

4. Use Figure 58 as an advanced organizer, guide, and recording device.

5. Discuss the implications of this information for use in classrooms.

Planning Instructional Strategies (Pages 84–87)

1. Review the planning process on page 84 of Gregory and Chapman, *Differentiated Instructional Strategies: One Size Doesn't Fit All* (2002a).

2. Compare and contrast focus activities and sponge activities using a Venn diagram (Figure 59) or a Comparing Two Things flow chart (Figure 60).

3. Ask teachers to consider the suggestions on pages 86 and 87 of Gregory and Chapman (2002a). Can they add to these based on their own experience?

Graphic Organizers (Pages 87–93)

1. Ask teachers to reflect on their use of graphic organizers.

   • How are they "brain compatible"?
   • Which ones do teachers already use in the classroom?
   • How do graphic organizers support multiple intelligence theory?

Figure 58   Advanced organizer for discussing how the brain works

Read, interpret, be ready to explain! Use examples where you can!	4. Attention
1. Memory	5. Rehearsal
2. Context	6. Emotions
3. Associating concepts	7. Recall and Rehearsal

2. Ask teachers (alone or working in pairs) to select a graphic organizer from Figure 61.

3. After the selection, ask the teachers to use the organizer they have chosen in relation to the concept of differentiation to further development of their understanding and continued dialogue. Examples:

   • *Fact Frame:* Write "Differentiation is important for students" in the center box. Write supporting details in the outer box.

Figure 59   Venn diagram used to identify an area of overlap between two topics

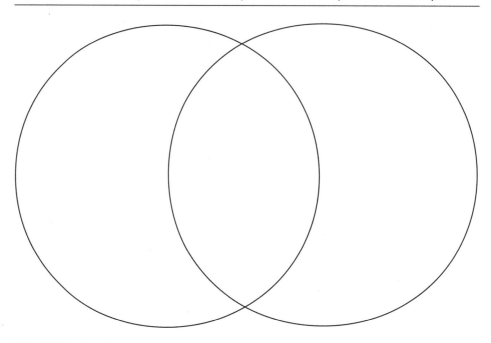

- *Roll It:* Write "differentiation" in the tire section. Write four key points on the spokes.
- *Inside Out:* Write "differentiation" in the center. Write its attributes in the outer oval.
- *Angle Antics:* Put "differentiation" in the big triangle. Write the effects on each side of the triangle. Put "traditional" in the bottom triangle and the effects on each side.
- *Star Connections:* Put "differentiation" in the center and one positive outcome on the points of the star.
- *Drumming Up Details:* Write a prediction about differentiation on the top of the drum. State the outcomes or learned facts on the side of the drum.
- *Facts and Opinions:* Write a fact about differentiation in the center. List an opinion by each arrow.
- *3 and 3:* Write an important topic (differentiation and traditional) in each of the large triangles. Write the meaning, write a sentence, and draw a picture on the sidelines.
- *Summing It Up:* In the top rectangle, write a fact about differentiation. In the next two boxes, write two supporting details. Then write a summary or conclusion in the bottom figure.

Figure 60   Comparing Two Things flow chart

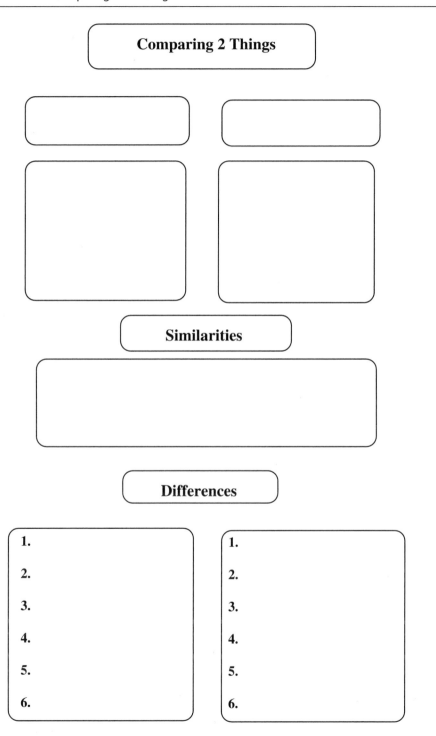

Figure 61   Graphic organizer framework

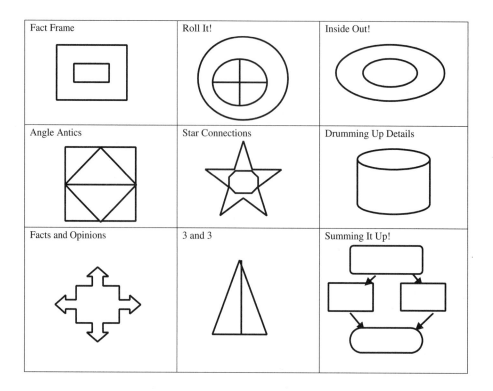

METAPHORS (PAGE 93)

1. Ask teachers to think about the use of metaphors as an instructional strategy. Using metaphors is also another way of using the thinking skill of compare and contrast.

2. Review Figure 31 (Chapter II-2) about learning styles and thinking styles and Figure 46 (Chapter II-4) relating adjustable assignments to a Slinky. The power of an analogy or metaphor is that the concept is understood and its attributes are remembered better when it is related to a well-known object or idea. An analogy is a single concept that encompasses a large mental file of information.

3. Discuss how metaphors and analogies can be used in the classroom to increase understanding and memory retention.

COOPERATIVE GROUP LEARNING (PAGES 93–100)

1. Provide teachers with a copy of the SCANS report (U.S. Secretary of Labor, 1991) and ask that they examine the necessary skills. One of the essential skills is the ability to get along with others and work as a team. Cooperative group learning is a strategy that helps develop effective social skills, increase understanding and retention, and facilitate higher-order thinking.

2. Ask teachers to discuss problems of students working collaboratively. As issues surface, time may be given to suggesting solutions to group work problems.

3. Review the TASK acronym (Gregory & Chapman, 2002a; Robbins, Gregory, & Herndon, 2000) and facilitate a discussion focusing on those four aspects of cooperative group learning:

   T Thinking is built into the process

   A Accountability is essential. Goal achievement: both individual and group

   S Social skills for team success

   K Keeping everyone on TASK: Roles, tasks, resources, novelty, simulations, and clear expectations

4. How do we ensure that the four TASK aspects are implemented when we use cooperative group learning as a strategy?

5. Suggest that teachers use Figure 62 to create charts and brainstorm ways to ensure that we attend to the essential elements. Post the charts and invite teachers to do a wall walk so that they can see what others have suggested.

6. Reflect on the steps and questions for using cooperative group learning on pages 99–100 of Gregory and Chapman (2002a).

JIGSAW (PAGES 100–103)

1. Facilitate a discussion about the jigsaw strategy and its uses.

2. Examine Figure 63 and suggest several variations that teachers might use for a character sketch. Or use Figure 64 on body systems, which may be used in a science or health class.

3. Invite teachers to work in groups of four to complete Figure 65 about differentiated instruction, focusing on evidence of creating

Figure 62   Implementing the TASK elements of cooperative group learning

Thinking Skills Are Built into the Process
Accountability Is Essential
Social Skills for Team Success
Keeping Students on Task

the climate, knowing the learner, assessing the learner, and adjusting assignments.

4. Challenge teachers to adopt or adapt this model for use with some topic or content in the next few weeks. Ask teachers to bring to the next meeting their sample plus examples of student work.

ROLE-PLAYING (PAGES 103–104)

1. Review the why and how of using this strategy.

2. Facilitate a discussion, focusing on questions such as:
   - How is it brain compatible?
   - How might it be used in the classroom in a variety of subject areas to increase retention and understanding?

3. Screen the video *Differentiating Instruction to Meet the Needs of All Learners,* secondary edition, Tape 2, at the 6–11:30 mark (Gregory & Chapman, 2002c).

4. Ask teachers to list all of the instructional strategies that teachers in the video have used.

Figure 63 Character sketch: Used as a graphic organizer when reading a story or novel

Character:

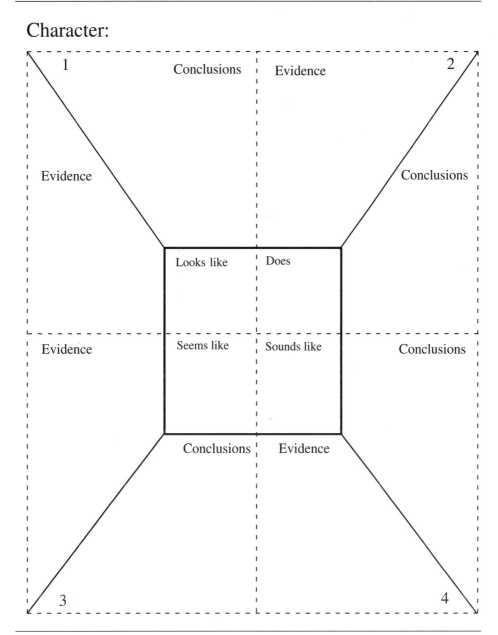

Figure 64   Body systems: Used as a graphic organizer in a science or health class

Body Systems:

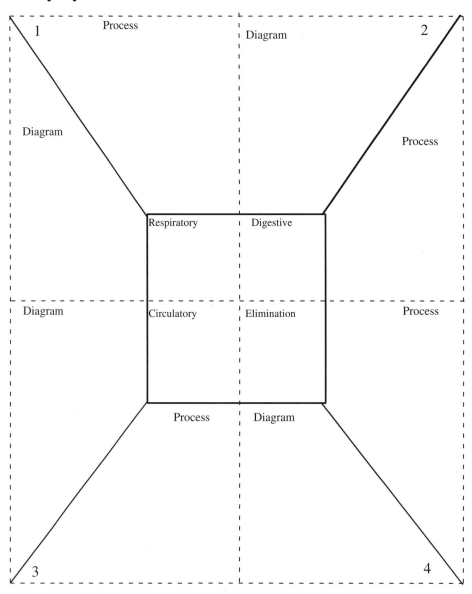

Figure 65   Graphic organizer for differentiated instruction

Differentiated Instruction:

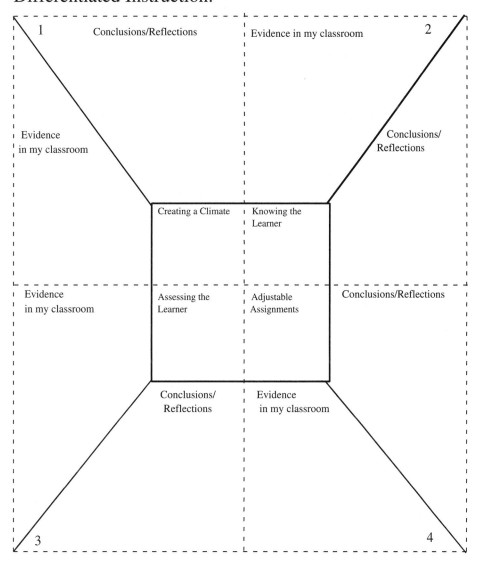

Chapter II-6

Curriculum Approaches for Differentiated Classrooms

CENTERS (PAGES 105-118)

1. Considering centers as a curriculum model, what concerns surface when teachers think about utilizing centers in the classroom? These concerns will usually focus on matters relating to design, management, and assessment.

2. Discuss these concerns, acknowledging that teachers who have experience with centers may be excellent resources for the larger group. It is often a great opportunity for middle and secondary teachers to be able to tap into their colleagues who teach in elementary schools where centers are often more prevalent.

3. Discuss *design* concerns: Remind teachers that they need to consider standards and content objectives before designing the centers so that the centers are real learning experiences and not just "fun" activities.

4. Discuss *management* concerns: Teachers may also consider and discuss the management procedures and techniques suggested in

the text (Gregory & Chapman, 2002a, pp. 107–112) and also share the techniques they have discovered work well with students.

5. Discuss *assessment:* There are a variety of assessment tools on pages 114–118, including anecdotals, checklists, questioning techniques, and student self-assessments with metacognitive tools.

6. Use Figure 66 as a Center Planning Template. Ask teachers to work collaboratively to design centers that will reflect standards and increase students' knowledge and skills.

7. Teachers may also use Figure 67 as a resource for multiple intelligences ideas and activities to incorporate in their planning.

PROJECTS FOR DIFFERENTIATED CLASSROOMS (PAGES 118-126)

1. Invite teachers to use the triple Venn diagram in Figure 68 to compare and contrast projects that are structured, topic-related, and open-ended.

2. Encourage teachers to examine the project samples on pages 121–122 of Gregory and Chapman (2002a) and think about how this model may be adapted to use in their classrooms.

3. Review assessment strategies, including rubrics, on pages 124–125 (Gregory & Chapman, 2002a).

4. Suggest that teachers also explore the RubiStar Web site that will help them custom design rubrics for their projects (http://rubistar. 4teachers.org).

PROBLEM-BASED LEARNING (PAGES 126-129)

1. Ask teachers to read the pages in Gregory and Chapman (2002a) about problem-based learning.

2. Facilitate a discussion about problem-based learning, including the questions:

   - What is it?
   - Why do it?
   - How do you do it?
   - What is it about problem-based learning that is brain compatible?
   - How can problems be adjusted to suit different learners based on readiness, interest, or complexity?

Figure 66   Center planning template

Center:

Standards:_____

Content:_____

_____

_____

Who: _____

Activities	Materials
	Location
Assessment	**Teacher Reflections**

Figure 67   Multiple intelligences planner for centers and projects

Verbal/Linguistic
Prepare a report
Write a play or essay
Create a poem or recitation
Listen to an audiotape on . . .
Interview
Label a diagram
Give directions for . . .

Bodily/Kinesthetic
Create a role-play
Construct a model
    or representation
Develop a mime
Create a tableau for . . .
Manipulate materials
Work through a simulation
Create actions for . . .

Musical/Rhythmic
Compose a rap song or rhyme
Create a jingle to teach others . . .
Listen to musical selections about . . .
Write a poem
Select music or songs
    for a particular purpose

Naturalist
Discover or experiment
Categorize materials or ideas
Look for ideas from nature
Adapt materials to a new use
Connect ideas to nature
Examine materials
    to make generalizations

Visual/Spatial
Draw a picture
Create a mural or display
Illustrate an event
Make a diagram
Create a cartoon
Paint or design a poster
Design a graphic
Use color to . . .

Interpersonal
Work with a partner or group
Discuss and come
    to conclusions
Solve a problem together
Survey or interview others
Dialogue about a topic
Use cooperative groups

Logical/Mathematical
Create a pattern
Describe a sequence or process
Develop a rationale
Analyze a situation
Critically assess . . .
Classify, rank, or compare . . .
Interpret evidence . . .

Intrapersonal
Think about and plan
Write in a journal
Review or visualize a way
    to do something
Make a connection with
    past information or experiences
Metacognitive moments

Figure 68   Triple Venn diagram to compare and contrast projects

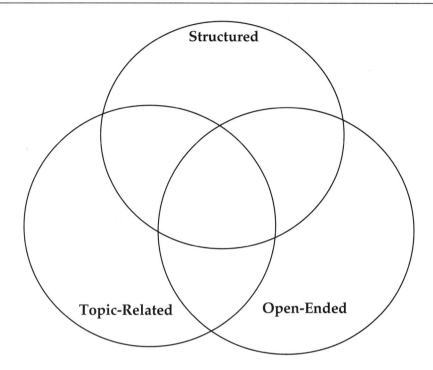

3. Screen the video *Differentiating Instruction to Meet the Needs of All Learners*, secondary edition, Tape 2, at the 37-minute mark, showing a secondary teacher who is using problem-based learning with students in a science class.

4. Consider K-W-L and K-N-D plans (Gregory & Chapman, 2002a, p. 127).

   • What do you Know about this problem?
   • What do you Need to solve this problem?
   • What will you Do to get what you need?

5. How might K-N-D be a useful technique to use when students are working on a problem?

CONTRACTS (PAGES 129-133)

1. Using 3-2-1 (Figure 69) as a guideline, discuss contracts and their use in a differentiated classroom.

Figure 69   3-2-1 guide for planning contracts

3 things I like about…	
2 concerns I have…	
1 idea I'd like to explore…	

2. Screen the video *Differentiating Instruction to Meet the Needs of All Learners,* secondary edition, Tape 2, 11:30 mark, showing a secondary teacher who is using Eight Choices for *Animal Farm.*

3. Examine Figure 70 for examples of how teachers can use Eight Choices to plan a unit of study about World War II.

4. Discuss how teachers can use a generic planning template (Figure 71) to design a set of choices for a topic they might want to use with their students.

5. Encourage teachers to modify or adjust tasks in the framework to suit outcomes, student interests, multiple intelligences, and available resources.

CREATING OPPORTUNITIES TO DISCUSS DIFFERENTIATED INSTRUCTION

1. Use People Search (Bellanca & Fogarty, 1991; Parry & Gregory, 1998) at any time for a faculty meeting or study group activity to create opportunities to discuss aspects of differentiation.

Figure 70   Eight Choices plus a Wild Card for studying WWII

1	2	3
Design four posters using your own drawings or pictures that depict the characteristics of life during WW II. Use captions to explain your visuals .	Develop an interview questionnaire; then interview at least four people who lived in this area during WW II. Describe at least five ways the war affected their lives.	Write and present a short one-act play that depicts life during the war, either at home or overseas. Use support material from novels or historical references.
4	**5**	**6**
Read a book such as the *The Diary of Anne Frank* and briefly describe four scenarios from the story showing how WW II changed the characters' lives.	Wild Card! Your choice Please design an option and present it in writing by _____	Produce a PowerPoint presentation using visuals, scripts, and sound to present life as one would have experienced it during WW II.
7	**8**	**9**
Listen to a variety of songs, musicals, and film soundtracks composed during WW II. Referring to the content of the songs, describe what the music conveys about what life was like during the war.	Collect a variety of pictures, newspaper articles, photographs, poems, and stories, and noting aspects of life during WW II, create a personal diary of how you would have felt growing up in that time.	Create a board game designed to increase understanding of what life was like during WW II.

Reprinted from *Differentiated Instructional Strategies: One Size Doesn't Fit All*, by Gayle H. Gregory and Carolyn Chapman. Thousand Oaks, CA: Corwin Press, © 2002. www.corwinpress.com

2. Give each teacher a copy of the differentiation review in Figure 72. Encourage them to walk around the room sharing answers for the statements in each box. They are sure to listen attentively to each speaker.

3. Remind teachers to write down the name of each person who gives them information. Those colleagues can become valuable resources for discussion and reflection as the entire professional learning community moves toward differentiated instruction for all their students.

Figure 71   Planning template for Eight Choices plus a Wild Card for any unit of study

Unit on _____
Choose one of the following options as a culminating activity for this unit

1	2	3
Design six posters using your own drawings or pictures that depict the characteristics_____ _____ Use captions to explain your visuals.	Develop an interview questionnaire, then interview at least 4 people who _____ _____ Describe at least five ways	Write and present a short one act play that depicts _____ _____ _____ Use support material from _____ _____
4	**5**	**6**
Read _____ and briefly describe four different scenarios from _____ showing _____ _____	Your Wild Card! Please design an option and present it in writing by _____ _____	Produce a PowerPoint presentation using visuals scripts and sound to present _____ _____ _____
7	**8**	**9**
Listen to a variety of songs, musicals, or create a song to the tune of _____ _____ _____	Collect a variety of pictures newspaper articles, photographs, poems, and stories _____ _____ _____	Design a board game to increase understanding of _____ _____ _____

Figure 72   Differentiation review for faculty meeting or study group activity

Differentiation: A Review...
Find a Colleague Who Can . . .

1. Explain why you think differentiation is important in today's classrooms.	2. Tell what part multiple intelligence plays in your planning for differentiation	3. Define focus activities and describe examples that you use in your classroom
4. Explain how relaxed alertness is possible in a differentiated classroom.	5. Define cubing and give and example of how you might use it.	6. Tell how a teacher's role changes in a differentiated classroom.
7. Complete the statement, "A differentiated classroom is like a _____ because_____	8. Share their thoughts about compacting.	9. Tell one thing that they can do to reach the diverse learners in their classroom.

Part III

Managing Change in the Professional Learning Community

Chapter III-1

The Implementation Process

FACING A CHANGE IN PRACTICE

In *Taking Charge of Change* (Hord, Rutherford, Huling-Austin, & Hall, 1987), the authors suggest that there are several stages of concern educators have when they are facing a change in practice of the kind involved in differentiated instruction. The discussion of the stages following has been adapted from their Concerns Based Adoption Model (C.B.A.M.):

- Non-Use, including awareness and information: Teachers usually don't know about the innovation and are not practicing it in the classroom due to lack of awareness or information.
- Early Use, including personal and management concerns: As teachers begin to use differentiated instruction, they have concerns about their personal efficacy and performance and about their ability to manage the classroom proceedings.
- Maturing Use, including consequences and collaboration: Teachers with maturing abilities in the classroom begin to look beyond their own concerns. They start to consider the impact the innovation is having on students and their successes, and how sharing their ideas with colleagues can impact student learning.
- Mastery, including refocusing: At this point teachers are reflective and evaluative concerning the process of differentiation. They are now

often able to "find a better way" through adjusting and experimenting with other strategies.

Often, in our attempt to implement new ideas we rush to inservice training and workshops, when in reality people need opportunities to dialogue about the concept and develop a shared vision of how the innovation would look and sound in their classroom and in their school. Figure 73 lists some of the issues faced during implementation and offers ideas for responding to these issues. Administrators and teachers may want to examine this chart and identify the support teachers might find useful at each stage of concern.

ADOPTER TYPES AND CHANGE

Everett Rogers (1995) and others have studied how an innovation diffuses through a group of people. People differ in their readiness to accept change. Some adopt new ideas quickly and run with them, while others take a longer time. Figure 74 describes the various categories of adopter types and suggests the different kinds of support each group needs.

Administrators may want to identify (without labeling) where people on the faculty are in terms of adopter types and look at focusing on the Innovators and Leaders who are ready, able, and open to differentiation. That is not to say that we won't worry about the Late Majority and Resistors, but we have only so much time, energy, and resources, so we had better put them where they will have the most impact and influence. To use a gardening metaphor: Don't water the rocks, water the flowers.

If we can engage the first three groups (Innovators, Leaders, and Early Majority), we have the potential to create a critical mass of implementers (52 percent) who will create a momentum that may engage those (Late Majority and Resistors) who have been less interested in differentiation. Continuing to engage the Resistors in dialogue may increase our awareness of where their concerns lie and may help us to help them begin the implementation journey. As Maurer (1996) suggests, we may want to walk toward the resistance so that we can better understand the reasons for and concerns about the change. Often, Resistors have seen too many innovations "come and go," initiated but not really implemented, and they may have become naturally skeptical about "this year's new thing."

A strategy to break down barriers that could be used at a faculty meeting is to have a reverse debate. Ask half the faculty (just divide the room with an invisible line) to brainstorm all the reasons why we should try differentiating instruction and how it might work. Invite the other half to generate all the aspects that would be negative and why differentiation

Figure 73   Faculty concerns about differentiated instruction

It is very important to listen to and recognize what concerns people have about differentiation and give them what they need to satisfy their concerns. As we begin the journey toward differentiation, it is important to listen to concerns and provide support.

STAGES OF CONCERN	EXPRESSIONS OF CONCERNS	SUPPORT FOR DIFFERENTIATION
Mastery *Refocusing* I have some ideas about something that would work even better. *Collaboration* How can I relate what I am doing to what others are doing	I've tried _____ and I'd like to do differently. _____. A variation of _____. Maybe we could _____ might be _____. I'd like to work with _____ to refine _____.	Help individuals access the resources they may need to refine their ideas and put them into practice. Respect the interest they may have in "finding a better way". (Hord et al, 1987) Develop opportunities for individuals to use the innovation collaboratively or to discuss applications of the innovation in collaborative settings.
Maturing Use *Consequence* How is this affecting other processes?	What difference is all this making to my students' learning? I don't want students to feel like 'buzzards and bluebirds' when I use flexible grouping. Has the climate in my classroom changed? How are students feeling?	Provide individuals with opportunities to visit other settings where the innovation is in use and to share their skills with others. Continue to provide positive feedback and support.
Early Use *Management* I seem to be spending all my time on getting materials and learning new skills *Personal* How will the new approach or process affect me?	How do I manage all these groups? Sometimes it feels like a 'three ring circus'. What if I lose control? I don't feel comfortable or capable sometimes. I don't have time for all the planning that this takes.	Provide help with the small, specific "how-to" issues that are often the cause of management concerns. Offer assistance with the logistical problems that lead to these concerns. Make sure individuals know that others share their concerns. Provide support and encouragement. Reinforce a sense of personal adequacy. Put individuals in contact with others who have managed the change successfully. Make it seem doable, bit by bit.
Non-Use *Informational* I would like to know more about it. *Non-Awareness* I am not concerned about it.	I don't understand this! Don't we already do this? I need more information. What do other teachers who are differentiating say and feel? Oh, great! This month's new thing. I've seen this before. This too shall pass.	Use a variety of methods to share information. Communicate with individuals and with large and small groups. Have persons who have used the new process in other settings talk with your group. Share enough information to arouse interest, but not so much that it overwhelms.

Figure 74   Adopter types and support needed

Types	Support Suggested
Innovators 8% Eager to try ideas, open to change, willing to take risks. Usually perceived as naïve and a little crazy and not well integrated into staff.	They need vision and support, encouragement and help with resources and materials. They need protection from the naysayers while they experiment. Opportunities to further investigate the topic and attend workshops and conferences.
Leaders 17% Open to change, but more thoughtful about getting involved. Trusted by staff and sought for advice and opinions.	They need articles and research that support the innovation. Visits to classrooms where it is working. Perhaps book study and video presentations for examination and reflection.
Early Majority 29% Cautious and deliberate about deciding to adopt an innovation. Tend to be followers, not leaders.	Partner them with a leader. Have innovators and leaders share ideas at faculty meetings. Provide time to collaborate and visit with others.
Late Majority 29% Skeptical of adopting new ideas and "set in their ways." Can be won over by peer pressure and administrative expectations.	Partner them with someone in the early majority group who is not too intimidating or zealous. Encourage peer planning, coaching, and teaching. Help them set manageable, attainable goals.
Resistors 17% Suspicious and generally opposed to new ideas. Usually low in influence and often isolated from the mainstream.	Keep them informed. Give them every opportunity to become involved at any point. Listen to their resistance and investigate their point of view. Share staff, student, and perhaps parent testimonials. Set expectations through the supervision process. Provide pressure and support!

wouldn't work. Then ask the groups to switch positions and brainstorm again. This is a way to legitimize the naysayers and also solve problems around some of the genuine concerns and barriers up front.

THE PROCESS OF CHANGE

We know that change is personal, both emotional and cognitive in nature, and even if we embrace the change, emotions will be part of the context of our process. Ken Blanchard (1983) reminds us that when people find themselves experiencing change, they often react in predictable ways. Figure 75 lists some of the emotions and feelings experienced by those who face change in the left-hand column, along with supportive responses in the right-hand column.

Figure 75   Emotional aspects of adjusting to change

Feelings as People Face Change	Supportive Responses
Feel self-conscious and awkward when they are asked to do something new.	Give people support and time to try new strategies until they feel more comfortable.
Grieve for what they have to give up.	Have a symbolic burial for the old ways.
Feel alone, even though others are changing too.	Facilitate opportunities for colleagues to problem solve and dialogue as well as share strategies.
Feel overwhelmed at the complexity of the change.	Help people to "bite off" manageable tasks that can be accomplished.
Are at different levels of readiness for the change.	Listen to concerns and support and encourage people with what they need at any point in time.
Concerned that they won't have the resources that they will need.	Help people find the resources they need and provide what is necessary to move them forward in implementation.
Revert back to their old ways if the pressure is removed.	Keep people focused on the innovation by supplying the needed pressure and support.

THE IMPLEMENTATION DIP

Even though we try to set up conditions that support and encourage change, it is still inevitable that we'll meet stumbling blocks along the way. Michael Fullan (1991, 2001) and others refer to this as the "implementation dip."

The implementation process generally begins with enthusiasm and confidence. However, people sometimes lose momentum or meet obstacles and challenges that slow down their progress or cause them to give up. All innovations will present problems during implementation, but the trick is to recognize "the implementation dip" and collaborate to solve problems and seek solutions that will help sustain the progress.

One creative principal organized a "dip party" when he recognized that people were experiencing an implementation dip. Everyone brought their favorite snacks and dips and problem-solved together to raise spirits and buoy up renewed energy to continue "working on the work."

Chapter III-2
Observation and Supervision

Encouragement and support are needed during the process of implementation. Evaluation should come later when teachers are further along in the process.

PRESSURE, SUPPORT, AND EVALUATION DURING IMPLEMENTATION

Saphier and King (1985) suggest that there are twelve cultural norms that support growth in a positive culture:

1. Collegiality
2. Experimentation
3. High expectations
4. Trust and confidence
5. Tangible support
6. Reaching out to the knowledge base
7. Appreciation and recognition
8. Caring, celebration, and humor
9. Involvement in decision making
10. Protection of what is important

11. Traditions

12. Honest, open communication

Principals who adopt these norms can support the creation and development of a positive culture for learning for adults and ultimately for students.

Seven Steps to Keep Up Morale During Implementation

Step 1. Be vigilant in finding things that can be celebrated. Leave notes in teacher mailboxes whenever you see an attempt at differentiating and meeting student needs.

Step 2. Recognize any gains and be sensitive when a teacher is frustrated or disheartened. Perhaps plan a "dip" party when an implementation dip is encountered.

Step 3. Publish successes in a weekly newsletter, post an accomplishment on the faculty room bulletin board, or honor teachers during each staff meeting.

Step 4. Collect comments from students about their reactions to differentiated tasks and use them to thank teachers.

Step 5. Present a certificate of effort or attendance at study groups or for staff meeting sharing.

Step 6. Offer to take over a class or a duty so that teachers have an extended planning opportunity or may visit another classroom or school.

Step 7. Offer resources to help and encourage teachers to try something new.

"WALKABOUTS"

As instructional leaders, principals need to be seen as knowledgeable about differentiation. They need to develop a shared vision and language with the faculty. Principals who are visible daily in classrooms heighten teachers' awareness of quality instruction and provide recognition and encouragement during the implementation of innovations.

Management by walking or wandering is another extremely effective way both to monitor instructional and assessment practices and open doors to dialogue with teachers. It helps to deprivatize the teaching process, and it lowers teachers' anxiety through informal interactions about student learning. A powerful video produced by McREL (2000) entitled *Principles in Action* features several effective faculties and their collaborative work in improving student learning. One example in the video is Debbie Backus in Aurora, Colorado, who shows her vigilance in focusing on student learning daily through interactions with teachers, students, and parents.

These informal visits and walkabouts help get a daily read on:

- Classroom climate
- Knowledge of learners
- Instructional and assessment practices in the school
- Professionalism of faculty

During the walkabouts, principals can enhance positive aspects of classroom practices by commenting verbally, leaving brief notes for the teacher, or sharing best practices noticed during the week at a faculty meeting. This is an opportunity to honor heroes, heroines, and risk-takers who are trying differentiated instruction. Everyone likes to be recognized, and it isn't long before word spreads about what gets noticed and celebrated.

Administrators may also inquire of teachers whether they would like feedback or data on some aspect of instruction or assessment that they are trying to implement, or data about a challenging student they are trying to reach. Data presented as information for the teacher to reflect on, respond to, or use for problem solving increases interaction with trusted colleagues.

Principals may want to tell the staff about the walkabouts and why they are important to the principal, the faculty, and the school as a whole. There may also be a specific focus for the month, for example, How is flexible grouping being used? Adjustable assignments? Evidence of a positive climate?

SEVEN WAYS TO FIND TIME

Time, of course, is always a scarce resource in schools, and administrators need to be creative in finding ways to help teachers collaborate with colleagues and implement new innovations. Many principals are quite creative in how they find time for teachers to collaborate and discuss their craft (Pardini, 1999; Purnell & Hill, 1992). Here are seven methods for finding more time:

1. *"Bank" time:* Some schools bank time by adding a few minutes a day to the schedule and accumulating a block of time for collaboration by releasing students early or beginning classes later one morning every few weeks.

2. *Early release:* Other districts have established an early release format, where each Wednesday afternoon students are released at 2:30 P.M. so that teachers can plan between then and 4:30 P.M.

3. *Buddy system:* Teachers can develop a buddy system for their students, teaming them with students from another grade level, so that when the two students meet one teacher can monitor the buddies and the other teacher can meet with his or her planning partner.

4. *"Grandparent" program:* Some schools have a grandparent program. This means that retired qualified teachers and administrators volunteer their time one or two afternoons a month in order to allow teachers to plan collaboratively.

5. *Community service:* Many secondary programs require students to engage in community service. If that community service can be coordinated so that students are all participating at the same time, then teachers can be freed to collaborate and plan for differentiation.

6. *Morning meetings:* If there is a high level of commitment, teachers may agree to meet for an hour or so before school starts once a week to plan and share ideas. (See also Bagel Breakfast in Chapter I-1.)

7. *Summer break:* Many schools with committed teachers also take advantage of summer time when teachers can participate in workshops or summer institutes, work on curriculum to embed differentiation, or team plan. This is a good time for teachers to focus without the worry of leaving their students or planning for a substitute teacher.

Some districts offer professional development credits toward recertification or graduate work. If possible, stipends may be given for extra time. This is a very good way to get the "keen teachers" trained to be a cadre of support and a resource for the school.

IDENTIFYING KNOWLEDGE AND SKILLS NEEDED

Teachers are more comfortable with any new innovation if they are clear about the *what* and the *how* of the innovation and the benefits it will have for students if it is implemented. In facilitating change, we have to be clear about the knowledge and skills that teachers need in order to be successful in differentiating instruction for and with students.

Teachers Should Know:

- *Facts:* Define differentiation and its importance (rationale)
- *Common language:* Content, readiness, process (activities), interest, products, learning styles, multiple intelligences

- *Expectations:*
  - Students are given respectful tasks.
  - Students are grouped flexibly.
  - Students are offered varied instructional strategies.
  - Students are given choices.

Teachers Should Understand:

- That all students are unique and they learn in different ways on different days
- That teachers are responsible for engaging and coaching students, providing high-quality interactions, materials, and environments within a clearly focused curriculum

Teachers Should Be Able to Create Learning Opportunities That:

- Target standards
- Offer relevant and meaningful tasks to students
- Encourage creativity
- Develop skills
- Allow for student choices

IMPLEMENTATION PROFILE

An implementation profile is very similar to a rubric, and we know how helpful rubrics are in keeping a target visible and attainable when we persist and take small steps toward continuous improvement. The profile provides four levels of implementation: Non-Use (mechanical), Beginning, Routine, and Refined (Figure 76). It is a continuum that administrators and teachers can use as a conversation piece to assess where they are in terms of each of the areas outlined as necessary for differentiated instruction. The profile helps faculty members know where they are and set goals for continued growth in the areas that are targeted for further improvement.

EVALUATION AND REFLECTION

Principals and administrators need to collect data during their observations and walkabouts so that a dialogue may take place with teachers to encourage reflection and to identify areas of strength and opportunities for growth. Figure 77 may be useful for collecting data in various categories.

Cognitive coaching strategies (Costa & Garmston, 2002) can be useful in sharing the data and encouraging faculty to reflect, project, and solve problems in response to the data. Figure 78 may also be used as a reflection tool for teachers. Its checklist of questions for planning differentiated learning will be useful as teachers begin to move toward more differentiated classrooms. It can help them measure their progress from time to time as they implement their new ideas and strategies.

The strategies, ideas, and templates in this book are designed to assist teachers and administrators as they work collaboratively to explore, examine, and implement differentiated instruction to better serve their students. This is a journey of self-examination and discovery and not a quick fix to learning. It is also not a panacea to the struggles that each teacher faces as she or he responds to a group of 20, 30, or more individuals in classrooms each day.

Figure 76   Implementation profile

	Non-Use	Beginning	Routine	Refined
Creating the Climate	Restrictive Lacking warmth Or student focus	Warm Engaging Openness Safe	Warm/fun Engaging Openness Supportive Safe Inclusive Enthusiastic Responsive	Student are in "flow." Responsive individually and collectively Encouraging risk taking Questioning Cubing
Knowing the Learner	No attempt made to identify Uniqueness of the learner	Students learning styles and multiple intelligences are explored.	Provides a variety of instructional & assessment practices to routinely respect styles & multiple intelligences of students	Through reflection and conferences with students builds on and sets goals with students considering their uniqueness .
Assessing the Learner	Test at the end of a unit	Consideration of standards & objectives Attempts are made to pre-assess using several methods of data collection. Test or presentation.	Consideration of standards Pre-assessment for planning purposes. Specific data collection methods based on expectations Choice of evaluation , presentation or activity to demonstrate knowledge & skills	Consideration of standards Pre-assessment for planning purposes. Specific data collection methods based on expectations Choice of evaluation, presentation or activity to demonstrate knowledge & skills Students use peer and self assessment techniques

Figure 76 continued

Adjusting Assignments	"One lesson for all" Total Groups	Students are grouped for a variety of activities	Teachers use a variety of flexible groups Heterogeneous and homogenous	Teachers use appropriate groupings Total Alone Pairs Small groups Heterogeneous and homogeneous
Brain-Compatible Instruction	Mostly "Sit and Get" One size fits all.	Teacher uses instruction based on personal repertoire	Teacher selects instructional strategies that are research based/best practices and continues to increase personal repertoire.	Research based brain compatible strategies appropriate to the learner and content recognizing students' learning styles and multiple intelligences
Curriculum Models	Mostly teacher directed lessons All students doing the same thing	Uses some projects and problems. More student centered	problems, inquiry, centers, contracts as appropriate.	Students input into the design of curriculum. All models are considered and their appropriateness for grouping, learning styles and multiple intelligences.

David Perkins (1995) reminds us that intelligence consists of a combination of deep knowledge within multiple domains, the ability to recognize patterns, the ability to consciously access a variety of strategies, and thoughtful reflection. As professionals, teachers should be constantly honing their craft with both the art and science of teaching in order to respond with intelligent behavior to learners' needs so that all may succeed.

Figure 77   Differentiation: Elements for planning observation

Climate	Knowing the Learner	Assessing the Learner	Adjustable Assignments	Instructional Strategies	Curriculum Approaches
• Safe • Nurturing • Encourages risk taking • Inclusive • Multi-sensory • Stimulating • Complex • Challenging • Collaborative • Questioning • Cubing **Team and Class Building** **Norms**	• Learning styles • Multiple Intelligences	Pre-assessment • **Before:** Formal Informal • **During:** Formal Informal • **After:** Formal Informal	Compacting T. A. P. S. Total Group Alone: Paired: **Small Groups:**	• Brain / Research Based Memory model Elaborative rehearsal • Focus activities • Graphic organizers • Metaphors • Cooperative group learning • Jigsaw • Role play	Centers Projects Problem Based Inquiry Contracts

Copyright © 2003 by Corwin Press, Inc. Reprinted from *Differentiated Instructional Strategies in Practice: Training, Implementation, and Supervision* by Gayle H. Gregory. Thousand Oaks, CA: Corwin Press, www.corwinpress.com

Figure 78   Checklist of questions for teachers planning differentiated learning for their students

B uilding safe environments

o   Do students feel safe to risk and experiment with ideas?
o   Do students feel included in the class and supported by others?
o   Are tasks challenging enough without undo or "dis" stress?
o   Is there an emotional "hook" for the learners?
o   Are there novel, unique and engaging activities to capture and sustain attention?
o   Are "unique brains" honored and provided for? (learning styles & multiple intelligences)

R ecognizing and honoring diversity

o   Does the learning experience appeal to the learners' varied and multiple intelligences and learning styles?
o   May the students work collaboratively and independently?
o   May they 'show what they know' in a variety of ways?
o   Does the cultural background of the learners influence instruction?

A ssessment

o   Are pre-assessments given to determine readiness?
o   Is there enough time to explore, understand and transfer the learning to long- term memory (grow dendrites)? Is there time to accomplish mastery?
o   Do they have opportunities for ongoing, "just in time" feedback?
o   Do they have time to revisit ideas and concepts to connect or extend them?
o   Is metacognitive time built into the learning process?
o   Do students use logs and journals for reflection and goal setting?

I nstructional Strategies

o   Are the expectations clearly stated and understood by the learner?
o   Will the learning be relevant and useful to the learner?
o   Does the learning build on past experience or create a new experience?
o   Does the learning relate to their real world?
o   Are strategies developmentally appropriate and hands on?
o   Are the strategies varied to engage and sustain attention?
o   Are there opportunities for projects, creativity, problems and challenges?

N umerous Curriculum Approaches

o   Do students work alone, in pairs and in small groups?
o   Do students work in learning centers based on interest, need or choice?
o   Are some activities adjusted to provide appropriate levels of challenge?
o   Is pre-testing used to allow for compacting/enrichment?
O   Are problems, inquires and contracts considered?

Training Resources

BOOKS

Cole, Donna J., Ryan, Charles W., Kick, Fran, & Mathies, Bonnie K. (2000). *Portfolios across the curriculum and beyond*, 2nd ed. Thousand Oaks, CA: Corwin Press.

Gregory, Gayle H., & Chapman, Carolyn (2002a). *Differentiated instructional strategies: One size doesn't fit all*. Thousand Oaks, CA: Corwin Press.

Rolheiser, C., Bower, B., & Stevahn, L. (2000). *The portfolio organizer: Succeeding with portfolios in your classroom*. Alexandria, VA: Association for Supervision and Curriculum Development.

Tomlinson, C. A. (1998a). *Differentiating instruction: Facilitator's guide*. Alexandria, VA: Association for Supervision and Curriculum Development.

VIDEOS

Gregory, Gayle H., & Chapman, Carolyn. (2002b). *Differentiating instruction to meet the needs of all learners. Elementary edition*. Sandy, UT: Teach Stream/Video Journal of Education.

Gregory, Gayle H., & Chapman, Carolyn. (2002c). *Differentiating instruction to meet the needs of all learners. Secondary edition*. Sandy, UT: Teach Stream/Video Journal of Education.

Tomlinson, C. A. (1998b). *Differentiating instruction: Tape 2: Instructional and Management Strategies*. Alexandria, VA: Association for Supervision and Curriculum Development.

WEB SITE

RubiStar. Web site that helps teachers create rubrics for project-based learning activities. http://rubistar.4teachers.org

Bibliography

Aronson, Elliot. (1978). *The jigsaw classroom.* Thousand Oaks, CA: Sage.

Bellanca, J., & Fogarty, R. (1991). *Blueprints for thinking in the cooperative classroom.* Arlington Heights, IL: SkyLight.

Bennett, Barrie, Rolheiser-Bennett, Carol, & Stevahn, Laurie. (1991). *Cooperative learning: Where heart meets mind.* Toronto, Ontario: Educational Connections.

Berte, N. (1975). *Individualizing education by learning contracts.* San Francisco: Jossey-Bass.

Blanchard, Kenneth H. (1983). *The one minute manager.* New York: Berkley Publishing Group.

Bloom, B. S., et al. (1956). *Taxonomy of educational objectives. Handbook 1: Cognitive domain.* New York: David McKay.

Brooks, Jacqueline, & Brooks, Martin. (1993). *In search of understanding: The case for constructivist classrooms.* Alexandria, VA: Association for Supervision and Curriculum Development.

Burke, Kay. (1993). *The mindful school: How to assess authentic learning.* Arlington Heights, IL: IRI/SkyLight.

Burke, K., Fogarty, R., & Belgrad, S. (1994). *The portfolio connection.* Arlington Heights, IL: SkyLight.

Caine, Geoffrey, Caine, Renate Nummela, & Crowell, Sam. (1994). *Mindshifts: A brain-based process for restructuring schools and renewing education.* Tucson, AZ: Zephyr.

Caine, Renate Nummela, & Caine, Geoffrey. (1991). *Making connections: Teaching and the human brain.* Alexandria, VA: Association for Supervision and Curriculum Development.

Caine, Renate Nummela, & Caine, Geoffrey. (1994). *Making connections: Teaching and the human brain.* Reading, MA: Addison-Wesley.

Caine, Renate Nummela, & Caine, Geoffrey. (1997). *Education on the edge of possibility.* Alexandria, VA: Association for Supervision and Curriculum Development.

Campbell, Don. (1998). *The Mozart effect.* New York: Avon.

Cantelon, T. (1991a). *The first four weeks of cooperative learning, activities and materials.* Portland, OR: Prestige.

Cantelon, T. (1991b). *Structuring the classroom successfully for cooperative team learning.* Portland, OR: Prestige.

Cardoso, S. H. (2000). Our ancient laughing brain. *Cerebrum: The Dana Forum on Brain Science, 2*(4).

Chapman, Carolyn. (1993). *If the shoe fits: How to develop multiple intelligences in the classroom.* Palatine, IL: IRI/SkyLight.

Chapman, Carolyn, & Freeman, L. (1996). *Multiple intelligences centers and projects.* Arlington Heights, IL: SkyLight.

Chapman, Carolyn, & King, Rita. (2000). *Test success in the brain compatible classroom.* Tucson, AZ: Zephyr Press.

Clarke, J., Wideman, R., & Eadie, S. (1990). *Together we learn.* Scarborough, Ontario: Prentice Hall.

Cole, Donna J., Ryan, Charles W., Kick, Fran, & Mathies, Bonnie K. (2000). *Portfolios across the curriculum and beyond,* 2nd ed. Thousand Oaks, CA: Corwin Press.

Collins, David. (1998). *Achieving your vision of professional development.* Greensboro, NC: SERVE.

Costa, Arthur. (1995). *Outsmarting I.Q.: The emerging science of learnable intelligence.* Old Tappan, NJ: Free Press.

Costa, Arthur, & Garmston, Robert. (2002). *Cognitive coaching: A foundation for Renaissance Schools,* 2nd ed. Norwood, MA: Christopher-Gordon, 2002.

Cowan, G., & Cowan, E. (1980). *Writing.* New York: John Wiley.

Csikszentmihalyi, Mihaly. (1990). *Flow: The psychology of optimal experience.* New York: Harper Collins.

Culture underlying attitudes can stop or start progress. (2002). *Journal of Staff Development, 23*(3), Summer issue.

Damasio, Antonio R. (1994). *Descartes' error.* New York: Putnam.

Deal, Terrence E., & Peterson, Kent D. (1999). *Shaping school culture: The heart of leadership.* San Francisco: Jossey-Bass.

De Bono, Edward. (1987). *Edward de Bono's Cort Thinking.* Baston: Advanced Practical Thinking.

De Bono, Edward. (1999). *Six thinking hats.* Boston: Little Brown.

Deporter, B., Reardon, M., & Singer-Nourie, S. (1998). *Quantum teaching.* Boston: Allyn & Bacon.

Diamond, M. C. (1967). Extensive cortical depth measurements and neuron size increases in the cortex of environmentally enriched rats. *Journal of Comparative Neurology, 131,* 357–364.

Diamond, Marian, & Hopson, Janet. (1998). *Magic trees of the mind.* New York: Penguin.

Doyle, M., & Strauss, D. (1976). *How to make meetings work.* New York: Playboy.

Driscoll, M. E. (1994, April). *School community and teacher's work in urban settings: Identifying challenges to community in the school organization.* Paper presented at the annual meeting of the American Educational Research Association, New Orleans. (Available from New York University.)

DuFour, Richard, & Eaker, Robert. (1998). *Professional learning communities at work: Best practices for enhancing student achievement.* Bloomington, IN: National Educational Service.

Dunn, Kenneth, & Dunn, Rita. (1992). *Bringing out the giftedness in your child.* New York: John Wiley.

Dunn, R., & Dunn, K. (1987). Dispelling outmoded beliefs about student learning. *Educational Leadership, 44*(6), 55–61.

Fogarty, R. (1998). *Problem-based learning and other curricular models for the multiple intelligences classroom.* Arlington Heights, IL: SkyLight.

Fogarty, R., & Stoehr, J. (1995). *Integrating curricula with multiple intelligences: Teams, themes and threads.* Arlington Heights, IL: SkyLight.

Fullan, M. (2001). *Leading in a culture of change.* San Francisco: Jossey-Bass.

Fullan, M. (with Steigelbauer, S). (1991). *The new meaning of educational change.* New York: Teachers College Press.

Gardner, Howard. (1983). *Frames of mind: The theory of multiple intelligences.* New York: Basic Books.

Gardner, Howard. (1993). *Multiple intelligences: The theory in practice.* New York: Basic Books.

Gibbs, Jeanne. (1995). *Tribes: A new way of learning and being together.* Santa Rosa, CA: Center Source.

Glasser, William. (1990). *The quality school.* New York: Harper & Row.

Goleman, Daniel. (1995). *Emotional intelligence.* New York: Bantam.

Goleman, Daniel. (1998). *Working with emotional intelligence.* New York: Bantam.

Green, E. J., Greenough, W. T., & Schlumpf, B. E. (1983). Effects of complex or isolated environments on cortical dendrites of middle-aged rats. *Brain Research, 264,* 233–240.

Gregorc, Anthony. (1982). *Inside styles: Beyond the basics.* Columbia, CT: Gregorc Associates.

Gregory, Gayle H., & Chapman, Carolyn (2002a). *Differentiated instructional strategies: One size doesn't fit all.* Thousand Oaks, CA: Corwin Press.

Gregory, Gayle H., & Chapman, Carolyn. (2002b). *Differentiating instruction to meet the needs of all learners, Elementary edition.* Sandy, UT: Teach Stream/Video Journal of Education.

Gregory, Gayle H., & Chapman, Carolyn. (2002c). *Differentiating instruction to meet the needs of all learners, Secondary edition.* Sandy, UT: Teach Stream/Video Journal of Education.

Guskey, Thomas R. (1994). Teacher efficacy: A study of construct dimensions. *American Educational Research Journal, 31,* 627–641.

Hanson, J. R., & Silver, H. F. (1978). *Learning styles and strategies.* Moorestown, NJ: Hanson Silver Strong.

Hargreaves, S., & Fullan, M. (1998). *What's worth fighting for out there?* New York: Teachers College Press.

Harmin, M. (1994). *Inspiring active learning.* Alexandria, VA: Association for Supervision and Curriculum Development.

Hart, Leslie A. (1998). *Human brain and human learning.* Kent, WA: Books for Educators.

Healy, Jane. (1992). *Endangered minds: Why our children don't think.* New York: Simon & Schuster.

Hill, S., & Hancock. J. (1993). *Reading and writing communities.* Armadale, Australia: Eleanor Curtin.

Hirsch, Dennis. (1997). *A new vision for staff development.* Oxford, OH: National Staff Development Council.

Hord, Shirley, Rutherford, William L., Huling-Austin, Leslie, Hall, G. E. (1987). *Taking charge of change.* Alexandria, VA: Association of Supervision and Curriculum Development.

Hyerle, David. (1996). *Visual tools for constructing knowledge.* Alexandria, VA: Association for Supervision and Curriculum Development.

Jensen, Eric. (1996). *Completing the puzzle: The brain-based approach.* Del Mar, CA: Turning Points.

Jensen, Eric. (1998a). *Introduction to brain-compatible learning.* San Diego, CA: Brain Store.

Jensen, Eric. (1998b). *Teaching with the brain in mind.* Alexandria, VA: Association for Supervision and Curriculum Development.

Joyce, B., & Showers, B. (1995) *Student achievement through staff development: Fundamentals of school renewal.* New York: Longman.

Kagan, Spencer. (1992). *Cooperative learning.* San Clemente, CA: Kagan Publishing.

Knowles, M. (1986). *Using learning contracts.* San Francisco: Jossey-Bass.

Kohn, A. (1993). *Punished by rewards.* Boston: Houghton Mifflin Company.

Kolb, David. (1984). *Experiential learning: Experience as the source of learning and development.* Englewood Cliffs, NJ: Prentice Hall.

Kotulak, Ronald. (1996). *Inside the brain: Revolutionary discoveries of how the mind works.* Kansas City: Andrews & McMeel.

LeDoux, Joseph. (1996). *The emotional brain.* New York: Simon & Schuster.

Lou, Y., Alorami, P. C., Spence, J. C., Paulsen, C., Chambers, B., & d'Apollonio, S. (1996). Within-class grouping: A meta-analysis. *Review of Educational Research, 66*(4), 423–458.

Lyman, F., & McTighe, J. (1988, April). Cueing thinking in the classroom: The promise of theory-embedded tools. *Educational Leadership*, p. 7.

Marzano, R. J., Pickering, D. J., & Pollack, J. E. (2000). *Classroom instruction that works.* Alexandria, VA: Association for Supervision and Curriculum Development.

Maslow, Abraham. (1954). *Motivation and personality.* New York: Harper & Row.

Maslow, Abraham. (1968). *Toward a psychology of being.* New York: Van Nostrand Reinhold.

Maurer, R. (1996). *Beyond the wall of resistance.* Austin, TX: Bard Books.

McCarthy, B. (1990). Using the 4MAT system to bring learning styles to schools. *Educational Leadership, 48*(2), 31–37.

McLaughlin, M W. (1991). Enabling professional development: What have we learned? In: Lieberman, Ann, & Miller, Lynne. *Staff development for education in the '90s.* New York: Teachers College Press.

McREL. (2000). *Principles in action: Stories of award-winning professional development.* Aurora, CO: McREL.

McTighe, Jay. (1990). *Better thinking and learning.* Baltimore: Maryland State Department of Education.

Miller, G. (1956). The magical number seven, plus or minus two: Some limits on our capacity for processing information. *Psychological Review*, 81–97.

Moye, Valerie H. (1997). *Conditions that support transfer for change.* Arlington Heights, IL: SkyLight.

Murphy, Carlene U. (1997). Finding time for faculties to study together. *Journal of Staff Development, 18*(3), 29–32.

Murphy, Carlene U., & Lick, Dale W. (1995). Whole-faculty study groups: Doing the seemingly undoable. *Journal of Staff Development, 16*(3), 37–44.

Murphy, Carlene U., & Lick, Dale W. (2001). *Whole-faculty study groups: Creating student-based professional development.* Thousand Oaks, CA: Corwin Press.

Newman, King, & Youngs. (2000). Professional development that addresses school capacity: Lessons from urban elementary schools. Paper presented at the annual conference of the American Educational Research Association.

Ogle, D. (1986). K-W-L: A teaching model that develops active reading of expository text. *Reading Teacher*, 564–574.

O'Keefe, J., & Nadel, L. (1978). *The hippocampus as a cognitive map*. Oxford, UK: Clarendon.

Ornstein, R., & Thompson, R. (1984). *The amazing brain*. Boston: Houghton Mifflin.

Pardini, Priscilla. (1999). Making time for adult learning. *Journal of Staff Development, 20*(2), 37–41.

Parry, Terence, & Gregory, Gayle. (2003). *Designing brain-compatible learning*, 2nd ed. Arlington Heights, IL: SkyLight.

Pascal-Leon, J. (1980). Compounds, confounds, and models in developmental information processing: A reply to Trabasso and Foellinger. *Journal of Experimental Child Psychology*, 18–40.

Perkins, David. (1995). *Outsmarting IQ: The emerging science of learnable intelligence*. New York: Free Press.

Personalized learning. (1998). *Educational Leadership, 57*(1).

Peterson, L. R., & Peterson, M. J. (1959). Short-term retention of individual verbal items. *Journal of Experimental Psychology, 58*, 193–198.

Pert, Candace B. (1998). *Molecules of emotion*. New York: Scribner.

Pinker, Steven. (1998). *How the mind works*. New York: Norton.

Powerful designs: New approaches ignite professional learning. (1999). *Journal of Staff Development, 20*(3), Summer issue.

Purnell, Susanna, & Hill, Paul T. (1992). The learner-centered school. In *Time for reform/R-4234*. Santa Monica, CA: Rand, 51–52.

Reis, S., & Renzulli, J. (1992). Using curriculum compacting to challenge the above average. *Educational Leadership, 50*(2), 51–57.

Restak, Richard. (1993). *The brain has a mind of its own*. New York: Harmony.

Robbins, Pamela, Gregory, Gayle, & Herndon, Lynn. (2000). *Thinking inside the block schedule*. Thousand Oaks, CA: Corwin Press.

Rogers, Everett M. (1995). *Diffusion of innovations*, 4th ed. New York: Free Press.

Rolheiser, C., Bower, B., & Stevahn, L. (2000). *The portfolio organizer: Succeeding with portfolios in your classroom*. Alexandria, VA: Association for Supervision and Curriculum Development.

Rowe, Mary Budd. (1988). Spring wait time: Slowing down may be a way of speeding up. *Educator*, p. 43.

Rozman, Deborah. (1998). Speech at Symposium on the Brain. University of California, Berkeley, March 1998.

Sagor, R. (1992). *How to conduct collaborative action research*. Alexandria, VA: Association for Supervision and Curriculum Development.

Saphier, Jon, & King, Matthew. (1985). Good seeds grow in strong cultures. *Educational Leadership, 38*, 66–77.

Sapolsky, Robert M. (1998). *Why zebras don't get ulcers*. New York: Freeman.

Senge, Peter M. (1990). *The fifth discipline: The art and practice of the learning organization*. New York: Doubleday.

Senge, P. M., Cambron-McCabe, N., Lucas, T., et al. (2000). *Schools that learn: A fifth discipline fieldbook for educators, parents, and everyone who cares about education*. New York: Doubleday.

Senge, P. M., Kleiner, A., Roberts, C., et al. (1994). *The fifth discipline fieldbook: Strategies+ and tools for building a learning organization*. New York: Doubleday.

Silver, H., Strong, R., & Perini, M. (2000). *So each may learn: Integrating learning styles and multiple intelligences.* Alexandria, VA: Association for Supervision and Curriculum Development.

Slavin, Robert E. (1994). *Cooperative learning: Theory, research, and practice.* Boston: Allyn & Bacon.

Sousa, David. (2001a). *How the brain learns.* Thousand Oaks, CA: Corwin Press.

Sousa, David. (2001b). *How the special needs brain learns.* Thousand Oaks, CA: Corwin Press.

Sousa, David. (2002). *How the gifted brain learns.* Thousand Oaks, CA: Corwin Press.

Sparks, Dennis, & Hirsh, Stephanie. (1997). *A new vision for staff development.* Oxford, OH: National Staff Development Council.

Sprenger, Marilee. (1998). *Learning & memory: The brain in action.* Alexandria, VA: Association for Supervision and Curriculum Development.

Stepien, W., Gallagher, S., & Workman, D. (1993). Problem-based learning for traditional and interdisciplinary classrooms. *Journal for Gifted Education 16*(4), 338–357.

Sternberg, Robert. (1996). *Successful intelligence: How practical and creative intelligence determine success in life.* New York: Simon & Schuster.

Stiggins, Richard. (1993). *Student-centered classroom assessment.* Englewood Cliffs, NJ: Prentice Hall.

Sylwester, Robert. (1995). *A celebration of neurons: An educator's guide to the brain.* Alexandria, VA: Association for Supervision and Curriculum Development.

Sylwester, Robert. (2003). *A biological brain in a cultural classroom,* 2nd ed. Thousand Oaks, CA: Corwin Press.

Taba, Hilda. (1962). *Curriculum development: Theory and practice.* Washington, DC: International Thomson.

Taba, Hilda. (1999). *The dynamics of education: A methodology of progressive educational thought.* New York: Routledge.

Tomlinson, C. A. (1998a). *Differentiating instruction: Facilitator's guide.* Alexandria, VA: Association for Supervision and Curriculum Development.

Tomlinson, C. A. (1998b). *Differentiating instruction: Tape 2: Instructional and management strategies.* Alexandria, VA: Association for Supervision and Curriculum Development.

Tomlinson, C. A. (1999). *The differentiated classroom: Responding to the needs of all learners.* Alexandria, VA: Association for Supervision and Curriculum Development.

Tomlinson, C. A. (2001). *How to differentiate instruction in mixed-ability classrooms,* 2nd ed. Alexandria, VA: Association for Supervision and Curriculum Development.

U.S. Secretary of Labor. (1991). *What work requires of schools: A SCANS report for America 2000.* The Secretary's Commission on Achieving Necessary Skills (SCANS). Washington, DC: U.S. Department of Labor.

Wiggins, G., & McTighe, J. (1998). *Understanding by design.* Alexandria, VA: Association for Supervision and Curriculum Development.

Winebrenner, S. (1992). *Teaching gifted kids in the regular classroom.* Minneapolis, MN: Free Spirit.

Wolfe, Patricia. (2001). *Brain matters: Translating research into classroom practice.* Alexandria, VA: Association for Supervision and Curriculum Development.

Wolfe, Patricia, & Sorgen, Marny. (1990). *Mind, memory and learning: Implications for the classroom.* Napa, CA: Authors.

Index

**CORWIN
PRESS**

The Corwin Press logo—a raven striding across an open book—represents the happy union of courage and learning. We are a professional-level publisher of books and journals for K-12 educators, and we are committed to creating and providing resources that embody these qualities. Corwin's motto is "Success for All Learners."